# A LOOK INTO THE SECRETS OF CREDIT REPAIR: HOW TO FIX YOUR SCORE AND ERASE BAD DEBT

## 6-STEP STRATEGY + 609 SAMPLE LETTERS TO TAKE CONTROL OF YOUR FINANCES AND OUTSMART THE CREDIT BUREAUS

### DIANA DONNELLY

# CONTENTS

# INTRODUCTION

*A hundred wagon loads of thoughts will not pay a single ounce of debt.* –Italian Proverb

We have all had that feeling of worry that manages to creep into your subconscious towards the end of the month. The money that comes into your account when you get paid often gets washed away as fast as a footprint in the sand as the wave of debit orders, debt repayments, bills, and other expenses rapidly depletes your briefly-healthy bank balance. In the short-term, it can feel like all you are ever working for is to pay off your debts and other expenses. In the long-term, you might feel as though your debts or current financial situation are leaving you with little breathing room to save for that dream home or new car you have been wanting to work towards. You might look up to successful tech geniuses or financial pioneers and wonder how they are so skilled at not only managing but growing their financial profiles. Whether you are Bill Gates or the average employee, your credit score plays a major role in your lifelong financial status.

If you are not working in or familiar with the financial industry, you are not alone in believing that under-standing the world of finance is daunting. Concepts like debt, credit, interest, and financial planning impact your everyday life, but you might feel as though grasping the details of how they work is confusing and almost impossible. This book will help you gain helpful knowledge on how these important financial concepts work, and specifically how to boost your credit score to be able to afford the things you need and to fund the lifestyle you have been dreaming of for far too long.

In order to pay for your daily needs and to save towards that big purchase or a lifestyle improvement, you have to earn an income. However, your income won't be able to pay for everything you need at once. For example, not everyone has the disposable income to fully pay for a house on the date they sign the sale agreement. Paying for these larger but necessary items like houses or rent, cars, appliances, and sometimes even clothes require you to seek out financial assistance in the form of taking loans, paying for items in installments, or applying for a credit card. This process of seeking financial assistance and making a decision about how you plan to pay it back can be very stressful and intimidating. Your current credit score might be preventing you from getting your loan, credit card, or mortgage application approved to allow you to borrow the funds from a bank or financial institution. The root of your stress might be that your low credit score results in you having to pay a ridiculously high-interest rate when repaying a loan. Studies show that 46% of people feel ashamed about having a bad credit score (Leonhardt, 2020). Your inability to get a loan might mean that you are forced to borrow money from friends or family, causing you further anxiety. At the outset, know that you are not alone in these financial stresses, and don't be too hard on yourself because the misconceptions surrounding credit scores are very common. In fact, 50% of American adults with poor credit scores have stated that they are unable to buy a home to live in (Leonhardt, 2020).

The useful practical tips provided in this book will give you the information you need to remove the stress and fear of the unknown from learning how to build and maintain a healthy credit score. Regardless of whether you are a single person trying to keep your financial head above water in a sea of debt or one-half of a married couple with dreams of a 2-bedroom home, pets, and a high-quality education for your children, the tips provided in this book will help you find out where the journey to financial stability begins for you. After taking the recommended action steps, you will no longer see building good credit as a 'necessary evil,' but rather as an important step in the path towards improving and uplifting your lifestyle, living the life you have always aimed for, and having complete control over your finances. My suggested credit repair strategy will put you on the path to being free from the burden and stress of carrying a high debt load.

Your journey to financial freedom has to start with an overview of the basic concepts relating to credit scoring. You will learn exactly what a credit score is, how it is calculated, and what is making your current credit low instead of improving it. The basics of first restoring or repairing a struggling credit score and then improving it will be covered next. A discussion of the relevant laws surrounding the credit industry is essential to provide you with a full picture of your rights and responsibilities as a debtor and those of the creditors you borrow from. An insight into the factors that credit lawyers and lenders or creditors consider when reviewing credit applications will be provided. The Simple Credit-Building Strategy will provide you with practical techniques that you can immediately implement into your daily financial life to improve your credit score. Negative aspects that might be lowering your credit scores, such as inquiries, late payments, and charge-offs, and how to remove them, will be explained. You will learn about the different types of debt and how to appropriately manage them. The meaning of the important *609 Dispute Letter* forms the final piece of the puzzle to demystify credit scores. Letter template examples will be provided with instructions on how and when to use this simple yet effective letter to save your credit score. The information provided in each chapter will empower you by giving you the essential knowledge to make an informed decision about your present and future financial status.

## ABOUT THE AUTHOR

From my more than 30 years of experience in various real estate positions, I have the knowledge to provide you with the essential information about credit scoring. I obtained my real estate license and started out working for a relocation company where I counseled employees and assisted them in relocating around the country. If the employee could not sell their home before moving, I would arrange for an appraisal of the property, and the company would purchase their home from them to give them enough funds to buy a new home in their new location. Once the company purchased the employee's home, I listed it and worked with an agent to market it until the home was sold.

After working in the relocation industry, I moved on to working in the mortgage industry, where I have gained 19 years of experience. I started out processing loan documents and ran my own company for years. I am now a mortgage underwriter working for an incredible company in Virginia. In this position, I review borrower documents for accuracy and completeness and ensure the loan meets all guidelines for loan approval so the borrower can have their application approved. I am surrounded by family and friends who underwrite mortgages, sell real estate, appraise homes, and research and prepare title work for title companies.

Working in the real estate and mortgage underwriting industries has given me an in-depth understanding of the issues faced by new home buyers. I have both financial knowledge and practical experience, and I am passionate about helping people break into what is a notoriously difficult market. My passion for real estate has only increased since I began working in the mortgage industry. I firmly believe that everyone should be able to own their own home, and I regularly witness the frustrations brought about by the bureaucracy surrounding credit scores. My goal is to help people navigate this difficult terrain and comfortably achieve their dream of home ownership. I am writing this book because I was once in your position of trying to wrap my head around improving my credit score to give my husband, three children, and two lively dogs the best life they could've had. I want to share the wealth of knowledge I have accumulated over three decades to help you gain an understanding of credit, how to improve your credit score and help you get the best rate on your loan.

## DISCLAIMER REGARDING FINANCIAL ADVICE

Before we embark on taking steps to improve your credit score, it is important to note that the information contained in this book is not intended to be and must not be understood as a substitute for financial advice from a professional who has knowledge of the facts of your individual circumstances. This book is intended for general educational and informational purposes only, and the author cannot be held responsible for financial decisions that you may make that depend on your personal circumstances. The content of this book must not be understood as a suggestion not to consult with a financial advisor regarding your specific financial situation. It is your responsibility to conduct your own research or seek financial advice from a professional based on your specific situation before making financial decisions. With this in mind, it's time to take that first step of investing in yourself and in your future by taking action to get a grip on your credit score.

# BONUS

**Want this bonus book for FREE?** Get **FREE** access to this exclusive book by joining my newsletter. Click here to join or for a print book use the QR code on the next page:

SCAN ME

# HOW YOUR CREDIT SCORE WORKS

## WHAT IS A CREDIT SCORE?

According to the Consumer Financial Protection Bureau (CFPB), one in five Americans in their 20s don't know their credit scores. This lack of knowledge is a contributing factor to why so many Americans are unable to get the loans and credit they need to live a happy life: they simply don't understand the credit system fully. The big picture issue is that you need a credit score to have access to legitimate financial assistance from a bank or any other lending entity.

Your credit score is a "3-digit number designed to represent the likelihood that you will pay your bills on time" (Equifax, n.d.). This means that one of the three major authorized credit bureaus, namely Equifax, TransUnion, and Experian, assess your financial history and use a number to indicate your financial stability, responsibility as a borrower, and creditworthiness to help lenders like banks, car dealerships, insurance firms, credit card companies, and other creditors assess whether or not to grant you a loan, credit card, or mortgage. If the realization has just hit you, yes, this means that your credit score has a major impact on whether you progress, remain stagnant, or deteriorate financially throughout your adult life.

Your credit score numerically ranges from between 300 and 850, and your creditworthiness is usually placed on the following score sliding scale: 300–579 is poor; 580–669 is fair; 670–739 is good; 740–799 is very good; 800–850 is excellent. A high credit score means you are more likely to have the lender's 'trust' when they assess your credit application because a high score means you are not a credit risk to the lender and the chance of you honoring repayment terms is very high. Your high credit score will make the creditor confident in your ability to pay back the money borrowed on time, and, in turn, you will benefit from lower repayment premiums, less interest to be paid back, or a more lenient payment plan.

Firstly, *having* a credit score is important, even if it is not great, because it gives you a basis to work. Those who are "credit invisible" have no traceable credit score and must start building one from scratch. Secondly, *knowing* your credit score is important because you can make informed decisions before approaching creditors or banks and know where you might stand in terms of the criteria they will use to assess your financial status. Your credit score can affect everything from your job, your life insurance, how you travel, and the roof over your head because it is a symbol of your reliability and integrity to people like employers, financial institutions, and insurance firms who have no other way of quantifying the potential risk they will be exposed to by dealing with you.

## HOW IS YOUR SCORE CALCULATED?

The three main credit bureaus mentioned above keep a file on you containing your entire credit history, financial commitments, and financial habits. A summary of your credit history can be presented by these bureaus in your credit report. The bureaus then input the information from your credit report into a system and formulas developed by the Fair Isaac Corporation to generate your credit score. This score is also known as your FICO Score, and it is the most widely trusted score by lenders because the FICO scoring system is the most commonly accepted method of calculating your credit score as it considers a variety of factors when generating your credit score. The concept of the FICO Score is similar to choosing to purchase a well-known and established brand of sneakers instead of a lesser-known brand. Lenders look to the FICO Score to assess your creditworthiness because they view it as the most accurate representation of you as a creditor.

Before your credit profile can even be reduced to a credit score number, you must have a financial footprint that meets the FICO criteria. First, you must have a credit account that has been open for at least six months to even show up on the FICO radar. Second, you must have an active credit account that has been reported as active to a credit bureau within at least the last six months. Lastly, you must be alive and well on your credit report. It might sound strange, but credit reports that indicate that the creditor has passed away are usually the result of either an error or identity theft.

Once you have met the criteria to be 'credit visible' to FICO, the scoring system will weigh up various factors to produce your credit score. Each factor or piece of information about you as a borrower of credit is weighted by FICO as follows: 35% of the score is made up by considering your payment history, 30% of the amount you still owe to creditors, 15% to the length of your credit history, 10% to new credit you have recently taken, and 10% to the type of credit you use (Timestaff, 2014). It's clear that once you are visible to the FICO scoring system, there is no way to hide your financial habits. This may sound intimidating, but it's actually beneficial to you as a debtor or borrower because having everything laid out in your credit report allows you to make better decisions about the type of credit you apply for and with whom you borrow.

The first step to repairing an ailing credit score is to check, double-check, and cross-check your credit reports with all three major credit bureaus. As a consumer, you are entitled to view your credit report for free, and you can request access to it by visiting the Annual Credit Report website. If you find any errors or incorrect information, you have the right to report this to the CFPB by lodging a consumer dispute through their complaint portal. Removing inaccurate information from your credit report can significantly improve your credit score. You should aim to check your credit report at least once a year, and you should check your credit score at least once a month.

Another way to improve your credit score is to draw up a budget for yourself, so you can assess which outstanding debts can be easily settled. Sometimes the rabbit hole of financial stress and debt can be very overwhelming, but simply pulling up a spreadsheet and populating it with your monthly debit orders and debt payments can be extremely helpful. You will have a bird's eye view of which debts you can soon unburden yourself from. Depending on your own personal situation, you can either choose to catch the big fish first and pay off those larger debts with higher interest rates faster. The other option is to pay off your smaller debts first and focus on the fewer larger payments later on. Both options might involve a bit of sacrifice and wallet-synching, but it will be worth seeing those debts crossed off your list instead of them staying there when new debts are added.

Increasing your credit limit is a great way to improve your credit score. Your credit limit is the maximum amount of the lender's money that you are allowed to spend on each credit card or other revolving credit account you may have. Having a credit card is a form of revolving credit because you have to pay a portion of the lender's money you have used back every month, with interest charged on the balance owed. Increasing your credit limit can show the credit bureau that you are a diligent borrower and are able to make payments on time. This method involves a bit more discipline than others because, for example, if your usual credit limit is $1,000 and you usually only spend $500 of it each month, you should increase your credit limit to $2,000 and either spend only $500 or spend $1,000 and be able to pay back the extra $500 spent on or before it is due.

Using a secured credit card can also boost creditors' confidence in your financial stability, and your credit score as this poses very little risk to them and allows you to make use of the credit granted while only spending within your own financial means. A secured credit card means that you secure the credit borrowed by paying a cash deposit for the entire or a portion of the credit limit. If you miss any payments, you will lose your entire or part of your cash deposit.

## WHAT HURTS YOUR CREDIT SCORE?

Before you implement these simple methods to improve your credit score, it is essential to determine what habits or situations are bringing or keeping your credit score down. If your credit score is between 300 and 670, it is likely that there is some action you need to either take or stop taking to improve it.

When you assess your finances, ask yourself if you are often missing, deferring, or skipping payments. Your payment history is the heaviest factor considered by FICO in determining your credit score. Missing a single payment or carrying over a high outstanding balance each month can drastically reduce your credit score, especially if it was healthy before you defaulted on a payment. If you are using too much credit, your score can come down because it means that you are more likely to miss a payment if you stretch yourself thin financially by increasing the amount you have to pay back each month due to spending. This is known as your debt-to-credit ratio or your credit utilization ratio, and it is a percentage that represents how much debt you owe compared to your available credit limit.

Closing a credit card account is another negative for your credit score because it makes you seem 'younger' or 'newer' as a creditor than someone with a credit card that has been open for five years, and this makes you a higher credit risk to the lender. Using or applying for too many different types of credit can also hurt your credit score because, although it is healthy to diversify your credit portfolio, it must also be financially viable for your lifestyle.

There are also seemingly invisible factors that can influence your credit score in a negative way. Your age, gender, and race all impact the level of access you have to credit, how much of it you are able to use, and how you are allowed to use it. Statistics show that in 2020, the average credit score of white Americans was 725, compared to that of African-Americans at 612 and 661 for Hispanic Americans (Holmes, 2021). Men have generally had higher credit scores than women throughout history, and 30% of African-American LGBTQ adults admit to having a bad credit score (Holmes, 2021). It is important to be aware of these societal influencers on your credit, but don't let them deter you from taking steps to improve your credit score.

## REPAIRING YOUR CREDIT SCORE: CAN IT BE DONE?

The short answer is yes. Your credit score can rise from the ashes of debt like a financial phoenix if you make the necessary moves to improve it. The key is to make sure to check your credit report regularly because the items on this report remain there for between seven to 10 years. Empowering yourself with knowledge of your financial status already places you in a better position than you were before.

It would be incorrect to put a timeline on how long it would take to repair your credit score to a healthy condition because everyone's financial situation is different. If you find that your credit score is not improving despite trying various methods to improve it, it would be worth your time to approach a credit repair company to assess your credit report, identify any errors, and start the process of disputing the errors and having them removed for you. There are laws and acts that exist to help you fix your credit score, and the Fair Credit Reporting Act of 1970 will be discussed in more detail in the next chapter.

There are many people who have been successful in repairing their credit scores on their own, as can be seen from the story of the successful blog owner, Becky Beach. Becky openly admitted to not knowing how to manage her finances, and she began burning through the money on a credit card she was provided even though she was unemployed at the time. She eventually found a job and made small contributions to pay off her credit card debt each month. She states that the payments took up most of her salary, but she managed to pay off the entire debt within eight years. Her credit score was healthy again, and she could invest in a property with her partner. She recommends exercising patience while you invest in healing your credit score and also disputing negative marks on your credit report by yourself or with the help of a credit counselor.

Now that you know that credit repair is very possible, let's explore the fundamentals of improving your credit score in the next chapter.

# THE LAW AND YOUR CREDIT SCORE

I n 2021, the average American had a FICO score of 714, which is considered 'good' and was a record national high in spite of recent economic and political turbulence (Horymski, 2022). The financial assistance and breathing room provided in some spheres during the COVID-19 pandemic allowed some citizens to boost their credit scores and save some of their income. However, even though 714 is a good average score for the population, millions of Americans still have credit scores below 700 and even as low as 550. If you fall into this category, improving your score might require a few lifestyle changes to reduce your debt, or it might simply require you to familiarize yourself with your rights as a consumer and a borrower of credit. Let's explore the law that regulates your credit score.

The Fair Credit Reporting Act (FCRA) and its important benefits for the consumer might be the spade you need to start digging yourself out of a pile of bad credit. Trying to navigate through wordy and complicated legal jargon that legal acts are often made of can be frustrating and time-consuming so let's simplify the main features of the FCRA and how you can use it to improve your credit score.

For contextual purposes, the FCRA was passed to attempt to balance the previous imbalance of power between the main credit bureaus and you, the consumer. Before the Act was passed, credit bureaus and credit reporting agencies did not have to tell you the reason why or the factors that contributed to the decisions they made about your credit score and financial status. These institutions were entitled to generate your credit report using all of your credit information, use it to calculate your credit score, and not tell you about any of it. The unfairness of this situation was noted by the government, and the FCRA was passed to give consumers new rights to access their credit information, but also the right to have it corrected if they believed it was incorrect. Because of the FCRA, credit agencies now have a legal responsibility to keep you, the consumer, informed about your credit reports.

The first set of rights awarded to you as a consumer through the FCRA involves access to your credit information, credit score, and credit reports. The FCRA gives you the right to limit who has access to your credit reports. It states that only authorized people or entities with a valid need to view your information can have access to it. People like your employer or financial advisor need your permission before gaining access to your information. Your privacy is protected with this right, and you are guarded against the threat of identity theft. The next access right in the FCRA is your right to access your own credit file that is kept by the three main credit bureaus. Access to this file is free and can be requested from any of the credit bureaus. The rules of the FCRA state that the credit bureaus must provide you with an extra free copy of your file and credit report at least once a year and at your request. Next, you are legally entitled to view your credit score with any of the three bureaus. This might cost you a fee, but, as we will discuss below, there are various resources you can use to access your credit score for free.

The second set of rights that the FCRA provides you with are rights of recourse, or rights to take legal action in relation to your credit score. Firstly, you have the right to be informed by your employer or by creditors when they use your credit information to decide to reject your job or loan application. Next, you have the right to have outdated negative information removed from your credit report. Credit agencies are allowed to keep information on your credit report for between seven and ten years. This means that any past information relating to you filing for bankruptcy, insolvency, or defaulting on payments must be removed from your credit report if it is older than 10 years. The last and most important right that the FCRA affords you is the right to submit a dispute relating to any incorrect, incomplete, or recent negative information on your credit report. If you submit a dispute or complaint to the credit agency that provided you with your report, the agency will have 30 days to either remove or correct the disputed information. This is the highlight of the consumer protection provided by the FCRA, and it all lies within the power of Section 609 of the Act.

## SECTION 609 OF THE FCRA

If the FCRA is your shield to help you through the battle against having bad credit, then Section 609 of the Act is your sword. The protection provided by the Act gives you a bird's eye view of your credit situation, but Section 609 gives you the tools to actually do something about it. The section makes it the credit agency's responsibility to ensure that the documents and information provided in your credit report are verified and accurate. This takes the burden of proof off of the consumer because the credit agency has to prove that they are right instead of you having to prove that you are not wrong. The credit agency must disclose all the information necessary to verify the information in your credit report when you file a dispute.

Section 609 focuses on "the consumer's rights to verification of accuracy, requiring the credit agencies and bureaus to verify and disclose all relevant information" (Millstein, 2021). Therefore, if you check your credit report and your score is on the lower end, or you spot inaccuracies in your report, or you want to try to remove negative marks on your report, you are allowed to dispute any information in the report. The credit agency must prove to you and to the CFPB that the information is accurate or it must be removed. Having these negative marks removed will instantly boost your credit score and place you in the black instead of continuing to build debt and staying in the red.

This might sound abstract because you can't exactly storm into a credit bureau and throw a book at them to fix your credit woes. However, we will delve into the finer details of how to use Section 609 to your advantage when submitting your dispute in later chapters. For now, the tip to take away is to check your credit report and credit score, to get your foot in the door. Secondly, using this knowledge together with a basic understanding of the laws in place to protect your rights puts you one step further. Lastly, using this knowledge and understanding together with Section 609 can rapidly repair your credit score.

## PUBLIC RESOURCES TO HELP YOU BATTLE BAD CREDIT

A bit of research and awareness about the types of credit information that will appear on your credit report, where to access this information, and whether you have to pay to access this information, is essential to repairing your credit score. Knowledge is power, and it will help you make educated decisions about how to build credit alongside debt and about your finances in general. The freely available resources listed and described below will assist you in putting the puzzle of your credit score and credit history together.

*AnnualCreditReport.com:* This website allows you to access a free copy of your credit report from any of the three main credit bureaus at least once a year. It is a legitimate website that is authorized by Federal Law and is supported by Equifax, Experian, and Trans-Union. Before requesting your report, ensure that you are on the correct website, as some credit reporting agencies will charge you a fee to view your report.

*Credit.com*: This helpful resource is a learning center that provides you with financial tips, knowledge, and information about how to successfully get a loan, mortgage, or finance a new car.

*CreditCards.com*: This site is handy if you're considering getting a new or additional credit card. It allows you to compare different credit cards offered by different companies. You can compare the interest rates you will have to pay back, the rewards programs, and whether or not the card allows you to transfer a balance. Customers can also provide reviews about the cards they have used.

*ConsumerFinance.gov:* This portal is hosted by the CFPB, so it's completely legitimate. It contains a database of credit card agreements from over 600 credit card issuing entities. It allows you to get familiar with what you are signing up for. You can search for a specific credit card company and view their standard agreement to make an informed decision before you sign up for a card. The site is designed to hold the consumer's hand through the often complicated process of understanding how credit cards work. Sections in the standard agreement are itemized, numbered, and explained in simple terms for the consumer's benefit. There is even a section dedicated to explaining the implications of taking a college credit card as a student and what students should look out for before signing an agreement.

*OptOutPrescreen.com*: This is the official Consumer Credit Reporting Industry website that is authorized by the Fair and Accurate Credit Transaction Act. It helps consumers process the request to either opt-out or opt-in to prescreened credit offers. This is when you receive a text message from a credit card provider because your credit history matches one of their offers. These offers can become annoying, and you will have to give the website permission to remove your information to stop the offers. Note that you will be required to provide your social security number, birthday, name, and address to confirm your identity.

In the next chapter, we'll take a look at how long it takes to get your credit score back up to where you'd like it to be. Bear in mind that your individual circumstances might be different from the advice and timeline provided, but they can be adapted to fit your credit situation.

# HOW FAST CAN YOU BOOST YOUR CREDIT RATING?

*A promise made is a debt unpaid.* –Robert W. Service

## WHY IS YOUR CREDIT SCORE LOW?

The CFPB estimates that, based on its data, a staggering 26 million American adults are "credit invisible," meaning they have no credit history and therefore no credit score (Gill, 2021). According to the credit bureau Experian, approximately 14% of people with a credit footprint have such low credit scores that they cannot qualify for a mortgage (Gill, 2021). These statistics are disheartening, but they emphasize the impact that repairing your credit score can have on your quality of life.

Based on the advice in the previous chapters, you have hopefully taken the step to check your credit report, scan it for errors, and review your credit score. A credit score below 670 is a cause for concern, but there could be several reasons why your score is so low, and it is essential to understand which of these reasons applies to your situation. A low credit score ends up costing you far more in the long term than the time and effort it would take to repair it because a low score means that you will automatically be charged higher interest rates and be subject to stricter payment terms and conditions on any loan or credit granted to you.

To move forward, you have to identify the habits or past credit events that are preventing your credit score from improving. Let's explore a few reasons why your score might be low, and you should be able to pick a few that relate to your circumstances. In later chapters, we'll look at solutions to these issues to accelerate the repair of your credit score.

The first reason your credit score might be low is that you have never had any credit history before wanting to apply for that credit card or loan. Communities of color are generally more credit invisible than white Americans because of past and present inequalities within the financial system. The system makes it difficult to even begin building a credit score if you have never had one, and this would significantly lower your score. Another reason for a low credit score is the mindset that one missed payment will not have any long-term impact on your credit score. The reality is the opposite, because ignoring your payments or paying them late signals major red flags on your credit report. A payment that is made 30 days past its due date can be a catastrophic red flag on your credit report.

Your credit card habits could be bringing down your credit score if you use more credit than you can pay back each month. A good rule of thumb is to use less than 30% of your credit limit on your credit cards to avoid your score dropping due to a high credit utilization ratio. There might be a default judgment against your name for a missed payment that you were unaware of or never paid. A "default judgment" is a judgment against a defendant who doesn't defend the case against them. This kind of judgment would show up on your credit report and bring your score down. Recent applications for one or multiple new loans, car financing, or credit cards can also lower your score because having more or new credit accounts means that you are a higher risk to the lender. Your low credit score could also result from identity theft or fraudulent activity where your information is being used by someone else to open multiple credit accounts and rack up debt, or if your name is being used to report on someone else's credit history.

It's clear that a low credit score could be the result of a variety or combination of different factors. Take some time to consider which factors might be affecting your own credit score and contributing to any blemishes on your credit report. This will help you find the best strategy to move toward improving your score.

## HOW LONG DOES IT TAKE TO IMPROVE YOUR CREDIT SCORE?

The answer to the question above is one that we all want to know, but it is also one of the most difficult issues to generalize about. There are many moving parts when it comes to your credit score, and all of these need to be considered together with your specific financial situation and your everyday life in order to place a timeline on your own credit repair journey. Importantly, there is hope, and credit repair is very possible, but what needs to be done and how long it will take is different for everyone. Avoid putting yourself under more stress and allow for a window of about 3 to 6 months where you develop and implement some good credit habits before you intend to check your credit report for any positive changes.

The first factor to consider before setting a timeline to improve your credit score is your mindset. Think about where you are mentally when it comes to your credit score. You might be overwhelmed and feel nervous about even looking at your credit report, or you might feel disheartened by how low your score is that you're not motivated to fix it. These feelings are normal and can be overcome by doing your research on the factors at play in your individual credit situation. There is always a solution, whether it be disputing an item on your credit report or adjusting your monthly budget to knock off a few of those credit card installments that are stressing you out.

The speed at which your credit score can be repaired largely depends on what needs to be done to repair it. This means that you need to take stock of your lifestyle, spending habits, credit history, and ultimate credit score goal to determine how long it will take. Consider your income, your disposable income, your monthly expenses, your spending habits, and all other debts you have to repay. Now consider what factors are weighted the heaviest when credit bureaus calculate your credit score. Your payment history is most often the factor that carries the most weight, so it is essential that you assess your debts and make sure you pay them on time, even if the payments are less than what is required.

Change your mindset to think like the credit bureau would when reviewing your credit habits and adjusting your financial priorities accordingly. For example, you might have two credit cards to pay off and have $100 in disposable income after making all of your regular payments, like rent, a mortgage, or your car install-ment. Consider putting $50 each into paying off those credit cards instead of putting the full $100 into one of them as this will be healthier for your credit score than leaving one credit card completely unpaid that month. Paying off your debts to repair your credit score can take about a month or two to have an impact on your credit score because your score will only be amended when your payment information is reported to and processed by the credit bureau and the credit reporting agency.

Analyze your credit report and decide which factor needs the most attention between your payment history, the total amount you owe, the length of your credit history, the amount of new credit you've taken out, and whether you should consider using more or fewer diverse types of credit.

Filing a dispute to remove negative items from your report can speed up the process of changing your credit score. Generally, credit reporting agencies have to investigate and respond to your dispute within 30 days of receiving it. If the negative mark is proven incorrect, it will be removed from your credit report, and your credit score will be adjusted immediately.

The successful credit repair story of Vicky Eves, a writer for a financial education blog that focuses on recovering from debt, will hopefully reassure you that you can bolster your credit score even if it takes time. Vicky states that she had let her debt get so out of control that she could not open a basic bank account because of the bad condition her credit score was in. After doing a lot of research, she decided to choose the solution of using a credit card that was targeted at consumers with bad credit so that she could make sure she paid off her installments every month. Slowly but surely, her credit score began to improve and was eventually completely repaired. Vicky's story shows that patience is key when trying to repair your credit score, and there is no shame in asking for help or finding resources to help broaden your understanding of the credit system. On the note of seeking advice, in the next chapter, we'll focus on some interesting tidbits that lawyers and lenders tend to leave out when speaking with you about your finances.

# WHAT LAWYERS AND LENDERS WON'T TELL YOU ABOUT RAISING BAD CREDIT

*Rather go to bed without dinner than to rise in debt.* –
Benjamin Franklin

So far, we have talked a lot about making informed choices and equipping yourself with useful information that can help you improve your credit score and help you live a more financially stable life in the long term. However, no matter how much you know about the inner workings of your own credit score, there are certain trade secrets that credit reporting agencies, credit bureaus, debt collectors, and lenders will not tell the public. Lenders are in the business of making money out of lending you money, so it would be logical for them not to reveal a few of their cards when deciding to approve or reject your credit applications. If you know these trade secrets, you'll be able to choose the best way to improve your credit score.

## WHAT LENDERS LOOK AT IN YOUR APPLICATIONS

When you submit a loan or credit application, you should expect the lender or financial institution to conduct a full investigation into your financial status and spending habits, and it is likely that they will focus on the negative things they find out if any. At the outset, know that lenders will look at more than just your credit score because this score is made up of what makes you financially reliable or unreliable. Lenders are most likely to first look at your credit history and credit reports since this is also the most important factor when calculating your credit score. They will look at any missed or late payments; delinquent accounts left unpaid; recent credit applications you have made; any balances that you still owe on loans; whether you were ever declared bankrupt; and if any of your property was ever repossessed by a bank. Your credit history will tell the lender how likely you are to pay back the loan and pay it back on time.

Lenders look at how long and what kind of job you've had when they decide whether or not to give you credit. If you have been unemployed for a considerable amount of time or if you have changed jobs too often for the lender's liking, then you might be regarded as a high-risk borrower. Your employment history is particularly looked at when you apply for a mortgage, so have an explanation and documentation ready to explain any issues that may arise.

The next aspect a lender will analyze is the amount of income you receive every month versus your monthly expenses. This factor can heavily influence the interest rate you are charged on borrowed money. Lenders consider your debt-to-income ratio to determine how risky it would be to lend you money and the chances of you defaulting on a payment. This ratio represents the percentage of your income that goes towards paying your expenses. Most lenders tend to prefer credit applicants to have a debt-to-income ratio of 43% or lower to take out a mortgage or finance a car, because this shows that you generally manage your finances responsibly, you still have disposable or flexible income, and you are not overwhelmed with debt (Luthi and Jayakumar, 2019).

Using the asset, you are applying to have financed as collateral is another thing lenders will do to determine your interest rate without telling you. If something were to happen to the car, house, or appliance you have bought on credit, the lender will weigh up their chances of recovering the value of that asset. Most often, lenders go off the basis that they will recover the full value of that asset, so they secure its value by charging you a higher interest rate and working that into the loan repayment amount.

The duration of the loan is something lenders will be quite strict about. A longer loan term means they think you are a reliable borrower. A shorter loan term means the lender is trying to keep their credit risk low and they want to give you fewer opportunities to miss any payments. Even though a shorter loan term might hit harder on your wallet, it is better for your long-term financial health to pay off the loan quickly.

Deposits or down payments are other factors that lenders consider when determining your reliability and the interest rate you will be charged on the money borrowed. The risk to a bank is lower if the amount you borrow is low. Therefore, banks will prefer that you put in a large down payment on the loan and reward you with a lower interest rate on the remaining balance of the loan. For example, if you want to finance a car that costs $10,000, paying a down payment of more than the average 10% of the total cost, like an amount of $3,000, is likely to get you a better interest rate. If your credit score is lower, be prepared to make a large down payment to secure a loan.

Lenders will look favorably on any investments or liquid assets you might have to cover their exposure to risk in the event of your inability to pay back the loan on time using only your monthly income. Your investments for a rainy day could help reduce the interest rate on the loan you apply for. These liquid assets can come from stocks, bonds, or funds invested in investment houses.

## THINGS DEBT COLLECTORS DON'T TELL YOU

We all dread that call from a debt collector asking when you'll pay back the money you owe. It's stressful and can be an annoyance if the debt collector is persistent. The best way to avoid debt collectors is to pay your debts on time. If they are constantly on your back, here are a few things you need to know about how they operate behind the scenes so that you can be more confident and feel less pressured the next time they call you.

Debt collectors will pretend to be sympathetic to your situation to get you on their side. It sounds like some kind of reverse psychology, but they know very well that you're not the only one with a sad story or situation. Debt collectors get paid and get commissions and bonuses based on how much money they get you to pay back on your debts. Therefore, they have an incentive to put pressure on you. On that note, it would be worth your while to check the statute of limitations in your state to know whether or not your debt has expired because debt collectors will conveniently leave this information out to get money out of you. Debt collection agencies buy debt from credit agencies for a fraction of the value of the debt and then attempt to recover the full value of the debt to make a profit. This means that they are essentially running a business and will do whatever it takes to get that money out of you.

Accredited debt collectors have the power to write-off a high percentage of your debt. They, of course, have targets to make, but they can also do the opposite and cancel your debt if you leave them hanging for long enough. You might have heard a debt collector saying they need to "call their manager" to get special permission to offer you the 'deal' or payment plan to help you. This is a psychological tactic similar to the concept of "good cop, bad cop" so that you feel more pressure to pay back the debt. They also usually call you at work to increase the pressure because you are more likely to be busy at this time. Debt collection agencies are using every bit of personal information they can get their hands on to find you. They likely have all of your personal information at their fingertips when they call. By law, in terms of the Fair Debt Collection Practices Act, debt collectors are not allowed to threaten or verbally abuse you.

## CREDIT LAWYERS

Credit lawyers are qualified lawyers with the legal knowledge, expertise, and experience to take your credit report dispute through the legal process, where they will fight to correct your credit score based on your individual and specific circumstances. A credit lawyer will assess your case, represent you in court, prepare and submit the required legal documents at court, and negotiate with the debt collectors on your behalf to find a solution.

Credit repair companies and credit lawyers are different because credit repair companies will try to solve your dispute using the usual procedures and they might only take it on if it deals with broader credit issues instead of your specific situation. Companies also sometimes lack knowledge of the legal loopholes that could really help your situation. Credit lawyers will comb through your information in detail and fight your case, within the boundaries of what you paid the lawyer for. Lawyers will take on more complex credit disputes and investigate them to completion.

It would be best to consult a credit lawyer if your credit report dispute claim is rejected. You might also need to consult a credit lawyer if your credit dispute is either too complex for a credit repair company to handle or if the credit repair company will not give you a personalized experience in handling your dispute. A credit lawyer might also be a more viable option to save you time in fixing your credit score as opposed to trying to fix it yourself after your dispute claim has been denied because you might not have the legal knowledge and/or don't have the legal authority to finalize the claim in court.

Finding a good and affordable credit lawyer can be overwhelming to think about at first, especially if you are already having financial troubles. It would be best to start with a debt counselor, who can also be a lawyer with knowledge of the legal process relating to repairing your credit score and reducing your debt. You should also check that the lawyer you are considering is a legitimately qualified lawyer who is experienced in credit repair matters and the related Acts before signing up with them.

## ACTION STEPS

In order to decrease your anxiety and increase your confidence about answering a debt collector's call, try to plan out a hypothetical conversation with one of them based on the behind-the-scenes information about how they work above. The language you use in this conversation could range from stern to questioning to indicate to the debt collector that you are aware of their intentions and the extent of your obligations.

For example, if they insist that you pay off a debt by a certain date, you could respond by saying that you are aware of the debt and it is on your list of priorities, but you are unable to pay off the entire debt by that date. You could also respond by saying that you have filed a dispute with the CFPB regarding that debt and it is still pending. If the debt collector calls you at work, let them know that you are aware that they are legally required not to call you during work hours because you have clearly asked them to stop.

It would also be worthwhile to consider what you would say to a credit lawyer if you ever decided to approach one to help you correct your credit score. When consulting with lawyers for your own benefit, it's always best to be transparent about your situation. Tell your lawyer everything, even the things that you might think reflect badly on your character, and have all of your related documents present the full situation. The lawyer is trained to try and either make these things seem irrelevant to your case or use them to your advantage.

# THE SIMPLE STRATEGY FOR STEPPING UP YOUR CREDIT SCORE

## THE SIMPLE CREDIT-BUILDING STRATEGY

Financial stress is unique in that it can feel truly hopeless, and trying to find your way out from under a mountain of debt or bad credit can induce this very unique type of stress. You might be under the impression that there's nothing you can do to improve your credit score other than practice good credit habits and wait. However, there are plenty of potential actions and strategies you can put in place to try and get your credit to where it needs to be. Following the Simple Credit-Building Strategy can help you see fast results and making good financial habits become second nature to you in your daily life. Let's unpack this practical gameplan so that you can take the steps to set yourself up for credit score success and eventually pay off all of your debts without going bankrupt.

### *Step 1: Check Your Credit Report and Credit Score*

The first step in every credit repair strategy, regardless of your personal financial circumstances, is one that has been a common thread running through the previous chapters: check your credit report and know your credit score. Just like how you wouldn't be able to bake a cake without knowing what ingredients you need, you won't be able to start planning to improve your credit without actually knowing your credit score. Checking your credit report means that you can scrutinize it for any errors and dispute them at the CFPB. If your dispute is successful, the error will be removed, and you will likely see an improvement in your credit report the next time you review it. Statistics show that 26% of consumers have at least one error on their credit report that could negatively affect their credit score (Dulcio, 2021). This statistic is even more significant when you consider that the credit scores of 20% of people who found errors in their credit reports increased after these errors were removed by filing a dispute (Dulcio, 2021). Checking your credit score is the first step in the credit-building strategy because, if errors on your credit report are the problem, then removing them might be all you have to do to improve your score.

Even if you are successful in removing errors or negative marks from your credit report, it would still make good financial sense to follow the remaining steps in the Simple Credit-Building Strategy because it will set you up to keep building up your credit score and eventually maintain a strong score.

### *Step 2: Draw Up a Budgeting Plan for the Future*

The next step in the strategy is to draw up a personal budget to give yourself a high-level overview of your assets, income, and liabilities. Those looming monthly payments might constantly be on your mind, so you might think this step is unnecessary. However, actually having a visual list of your monthly budget can make a major difference in how you manage your credit and your finances in general. Creating and sticking to a budgeting plan means leaving no financial stone unturned. You need to write down all the income you receive per month, and then list every payment you need to make next to it and subtract these payments from your income. If you are left with a negative balance, you know that you either need to make some minor changes in your lifestyle to be able to make your monthly payments or you need to set a timeline for how long you plan to maintain a negative balance until your debts are paid off.

Drawing up a budgeting plan, prioritizing your debts, and setting payment reminders can also help you keep your debt-to-credit ratio in check. This is also known as your credit utilization ratio, and it can impact your credit score if you are using more credit in a month than you are able to pay back. You need to allow yourself to have a view of the bigger picture of your credit habits so that you know how much credit you can actually afford to spend while still being able to pay it back on time.

### STEP 3: *Prioritize Your Debts*

This takes us to the next step of the strategy: Prioritizing your debts and being strategic in how you pay off each debt. Base it on how you have prioritized your debts in your monthly budget. Pay off your largest and most important debts first each month. These would include your mortgage, car loan, and credit cards.

### Step 4: *Set Up Payment Reminders*

Set up payment reminders to make sure that you pay your debts on time every month. Just like how you use a calendar to schedule your work or school diary and deadlines, set up a calendar or an alarm system on your cell phone to remind you to make each payment. For example, you get paid on the 25th of each month, you've drawn up your budget, and you've placed your car installment at the very top of your list and the clothing account you hardly use at the bottom of your list of priorities. The smart thing to do would be to schedule the car installment to be paid on the 26th as soon as you get paid your salary because this is a priority. The clothing account can be paid on the 1st of the next month, after your other priority payments have been paid, or before you get paid on the 25th with any money you have left in your account before it is resuscitated with your salary.

### Step 5: Contact Your Creditors

The next step in the "simple credit-building strategy" is to contact your creditors or lenders. This might sound impossible, and you might not want to risk exposing the fact that you have defaulted on payments, but you can rest assured that creditors are very much aware of when you miss a payment. They have the authority to pull up your entire payment history and to hunt you down if you miss a payment. However, you should be more scared of the impact of continuous missed payments on your credit score than of having a conversation with your creditors. Your creditors will appreciate you being proactive and transparent about any missed or potentially missed payments and will likely give you the opportunity to collaborate with them to create a payment plan that works for both parties. This will prevent the missed payments you've missed from accumulating to create a larger and unmanageable debt.

### Step 6: Diversify Your Finances

The final step in the strategy is to diversify your credit by making informed choices about the type and amount of credit you take on. Consider the types of credit you currently have and the debts you are currently trying to pay off. A good credit score requires a good credit mix, meaning that having six similar credit cards and no other credit might leave you with an average credit score, while having a mortgage, car installment, credit cards, and one other loan where all of these debts are paid each month will likely give you a good to very good credit score. You should also be careful before applying for new credit. Applications for many new credit types mean you are considered a "young borrower," making you seem like a high-risk borrower to lenders. It will lower your credit score, so it is important to know the difference between diversifying your credit mix and applying for new credit.

The Simple Credit-Building Strategy gets its foundation from the factors the FICO weighs up to generate your credit score. As a reminder, these factors and their corresponding weights on your credit score are as follows: payment history (35%), amounts owed (30%), credit history length (15%), credit mix (10%), and new credit (10%). You can relate every step of the strategy to a factor that is used to create your credit score. Therefore, it is a proven strategy to improve your credit score because it enables you to change the relevant aspects of your credit history that credit bureaus actually look at.

The relationship between the components of your credit score and the steps required to implement the strategy can be summarized as follows:

1. Payment history: To improve this, you need to know your credit score and have sight of your credit report. This component also arcs over the entire Simple Credit-Building Strategy because paying your bills and paying them on time is the original fool-proof way to improve your credit score.
2. Balance still owed: Drawing up a budgeting plan that you stick to is the key to working out how much you still owe and which payments are overdue.
3. Credit history length: Prioritizing your debts, daily payment reminders, and contacting your creditors will help you pay off your debts faster. The key here is not to have a short credit history but to have a long and consistent credit history where you have been paying off your credit on time.

4. Credit mix: This is where correctly diversifying your credit portfolio can help improve your credit score. The different types of credit you currently have should be prioritized with a timeline of when they will be paid off.

5. New credit: Improving this part of your credit score means carefully thinking about it before you submit an application for new credit. Credit bureaus will not give you a good credit score if you apply for many different types of new credit in a short space of time, and lenders will consider you a high risk.

## ACTION STEPS

Now that you have the solid foundations of the Simple Credit-Building Strategy, think about when you can start applying them to your personal financial situation. Consider the actions you've already taken to pay off your debts and decide if there are any opportunities to change what you've been doing or add additional steps to strengthen your strategy using the strategy above. A good place to start would be to request your credit report and check your credit score for free from a site like AnnualCreditReport.com so that you know the base score you are starting with. Next, take an afternoon or evening to draw up your budget and brainstorm where you can cut a few corners to pay off those debts that are your highest priority. If you can financially afford to diversify your credit mix, consider making some long-term changes like taking out a mortgage instead of paying rent. A mortgage can directly improve your credit score if you are able to make the payments on time and at the required amount. In the next chapter, we'll get into the granular details of improving your credit score and look at some specific tactics you can apply to your own financial situation.

# THE TOP TECHNIQUES FOR BUILDING BETTER CREDIT FAST

*Procrastination is like a credit card: it's a lot of fun until you get the bill.* –Christopher Parker

N ow that you have a solid strategy outlined to start either repairing or building up your credit score from scratch, it's time to delve into the details of what you actually have to do on a daily or monthly financial basis to succeed with this strategy. Some of these practical tips involve taking the less conventional route with your finances. It's all about finding a balance between those five factors that the credit bureaus use to generate your credit score. Remember to always consider your personal financial situation before using these tips in your daily life.

## DON'T CLOSE NEW CREDIT CARD ACCOUNTS

You might be so frustrated with your current credit situation that all you want to do is start afresh on a clean slate. If you're thinking that this "clean slate" comes in the form of a brand new credit card, hold on before you take that pair of scissors to the old credit card that initially landed you in debt. No matter how much disdain you look at that credit card with, trying to burn a hole through it for enticing you to spend beyond your means and rack up large debts to pay back, the debt will never go away. Closing your credit card to avoid paying your debt or because you feel as though you can never catch up on missed payments is like moving your unfolded laundry from your bed to that chair in the corner of your bedroom: it's still there, and it still needs to be dealt with. Even if you have good reasons to close your credit card, like maybe you don't want that specific credit card account anymore, closing the account can harm your credit score.

Looking at the positives of keeping your credit cards open will highlight the flipside, or the reasons why closing them will hurt your score. Keeping your credit cards open means that you lengthen your credit history and your credit age. These are both factors considered when creating your credit score, and lenders don't like to take on new or young borrowers because the risk of them not making payments on time is higher. Even if you owe a large balance on your credit cards, leaving them open and paying most of them on time will increase the consistency of your payment history, and this is the most important factor used to generate your credit score. If you have multiple credit cards and want to downsize to a single card, pause before you close the others because your mix or variety of credit is also considered when determining your credit score. Having multiple cards open also means that your debt-to-credit ratio, or credit utilization ratio, will be lower. This translates to you being able to comfortably pay back the credit you are using, and you are not over-using credit. This also shows you as a reliable and low-risk borrower. If you downsize to one card, the ratio will increase because you are using more credit from the only account you will be assessed on.

If you close a credit card that still has a balance on it, it will reflect as if you have used up all of the credit on the card because the credit limit and the available credit on the card will be brought down to zero. This can harm your credit score by increasing your debt-to-credit ratio. If you really want to close a credit card, make sure it doesn't have an available balance and that you write to the credit card company to close the card and report it as "Closed."

## USE AUTOPAY WHERE POSSIBLE TO AVOID MISSED PAYMENTS

This is a sure-fire way to pay your bills on time while improving your payment history with the credit bureau, showing up as a dependable and consistent borrower. On-time payments are a catalyst to a better credit score. 'Autopay' is another way to describe an automatic payment or a debit order. It's a scheduled payment that you set up to come off your account on a certain date to pay your bills. These scheduled payments can be easily set up on most banking apps or even by going into the bank and speaking to a consultant. Use this method to pay off your rent, mortgage payment, a set amount on your credit card balance each month, utilities, or your child's school fees.

The trick to using autopay to improve your credit score is to schedule the payments to go off on the right date. You should schedule the payments to come off your account on a date before the payment is actually due.

This shows responsible credit habits, helps your payment history, and depletes the balance owed. Setting up the payments to go off before their due date also takes into account the time it takes for the payment to actually be processed and to be reflected in your account. Automatic payments help you develop good budgeting habits because you are being responsible by paying off the essentials before spending.

## INCREASE YOUR CREDIT LIMIT

Before you increase your credit limit, take a look at how much you currently owe and how much credit you have left. Some banks will require your credit card account to reach a certain age before you are able to increase your credit limit because they want to avoid taking on the risk of you not paying the money back. An older account means a more reliable borrower. Others will jump at the chance of offering you a credit limit increase because using more credit means you will owe them more back and they can charge you more interest on the amount owed. You should definitely increase your credit limit if you can pay off your credit card installment in full when it's due every month. Also, consider increasing your limit if your debt-to-credit ratio is below 30% because it will improve your credit score by showing consistency and responsible spending. To calculate this ratio, you need to divide the amount of credit you've spent by your available credit limit. For example, if you have 2 credit cards with a credit limit of $2,500 each, your total available credit limit is $5,000. You've spent $300 on each card this month, meaning you've spent $600 of your total credit limit. Your debt-to-credit ratio will be 12%.

## CREDIT PIGGYBACKING

This method is especially helpful if you are credit-invisible and need to build your credit score from scratch. Credit piggybacking means you have permission to use someone else's credit card account to build up your credit score. You will want to choose someone you trust, and someone who has good credit because becoming an authorized user on someone else's account means that you also adopt their credit history, which will reflect on your credit report. You become joined at the credit hip, so to speak, and take on the good and bad parts of this person's credit file. If they have a solid credit mix, you get this too, and if they miss payments, it will bring down your credit score too. If you're considering this option to improve your credit score, be mindful that it is a risky solution that should never be taken on as a permanent solution to your credit problems. You are at a high risk of being scammed and left with an even worse credit score than you started with because you are giving someone access to your financial and personal information. If you are close to the person you are piggybacking off of, your relationship could suffer if you hit financial hard times during this arrangement. Most importantly, using another person's credit file will not help you make long-term positive changes to your financial habits.

## ADDRESS ANY NEGATIVES IN YOUR CREDIT REPORT

Disputing errors in your credit report is a foolproof way to improve your credit score if you are willing to make the effort. If you have a bad credit score, you have nothing to lose by scrutinizing your credit report and trying to get any errors removed on the chance that your score will increase. Over the years, the credit bureaus and credit reporting agencies have discovered certain errors that are common for consumers to find in their reports, and having a list of these at hand while you look over your report can be a light at the end of the credit hell tunnel.

Your report might show credit accounts where either the balance you owe or your available credit limit is incorrect. This makes your debt-to-credit ratio increase and makes it seem like you are spending more than you can pay, bringing down your score. The report could also have errors about your identity. Your personal information like your name, contact details, and address might be wrong, your identity has been used fraudulently, or your account details or credit history have been mixed up with someone else's. Other possible errors include transaction data errors where transactions are repeated incorrectly, or the status of your account could have been erroneously reported. For example, the report could say that you missed payments when you have proof that you paid on time or that you have closed an account that is still showing as active in your report.

## DON'T APPLY TO MULTIPLE CREDIT CARDS AT ONCE

Doing this will hurt the component of your credit score that's made up of "new credit." You will reflect as unreliable, inconsistent, desperate, and a young borrower to credit bureaus and to creditors if you apply for new credit cards often or if you apply for multiple credit cards at once. Each lender you apply to might think that you have been rejected by many other lenders, and this will raise their suspicions that you are unable to pay your debts. Before you send out many applications in the hope of one creditor taking the bait and giving you a chance, take a step back and assess what the best option is for you. Comparing the rewards systems on credit cards is especially helpful to convince you to choose the right one to start out with. You could also give yourself a timeline to make sure you pay off one credit card over a year or 6 months before applying for your second one.

## PUT YOUR NAME ON UTILITY BILLS AND OTHER BILLS

Being a homeowner is much better for your credit score than paying rent because a mortgage payment has the house you're paying off attached as collateral if you default on payments. Paying rent is almost a "credit invisible" activity because the payments go to your landlord and are not necessarily recorded by credit bureaus as part of your payment history. Of course, in today's tough and unpredictable economy, not everyone can sign a mortgage and become a home-owner. To reap the benefits of paying your rent and utilities on time for your credit score, you need to use rent-reporting services and source platforms that allow you to report your rental, cell phone, and utility payments to the three major credit bureaus. Research your options because some platforms might require steps to be taken by your landlord or they might charge a fee for the reporting. The updated versions of the FICO score and the VantageScore credit scoring system allow you to use your rent payments to be reported as part of your credit score. Your payment history will benefit from this, and your credit score will improve if you pay in full and on time.

## ACTION STEPS

You have to start somewhere, so select any of the above techniques that you think can help your credit situation. Consider how you can integrate them into the details of your overall credit-building strategy. Understanding the balance between how much you spend and how much you can pay back is key to finding which of these techniques will work for you. In the next chapter, we'll go through each step of the process of improving your credit score, decreasing your debt, and positively changing your financial habits.

# HOW TO RESTORE YOUR CREDIT SCORE: 10 STEPS TO FINANCIAL FREEDOM

A ccording to credit card experts, Steven Dashiell and Megan Horner, the total credit card debt in the US currently stands at $887 billion, which means an average of $3540 per American (Dashiell & Horner, 2022). Most Americans have at least two credit cards, and 51% of credit card holders increased their credit limit because of the COVID-19 pandemic (Dashiell & Horner, 2022). So, if you're one of the millions of Americans carrying a credit card balance or who owes lots of money in other forms of debt, then following the 10 steps below will help you get back on track to paying off your debts, rebuilding your credit score, and flipping your mindset from paying off debt to growing your money.

*Honesty is the best policy*: Get a hold of a copy of your credit report, sit down, take a deep breath, and calculate your actual outstanding balance. How much do you actually owe? Ask yourself if the amount is reasonable or if you should be concerned. Think about how many payments you've missed and how this might impact the "payment history" factor of your credit score. The sooner you are honest with yourself about your credit report, the sooner you can figure out a solution. The longer you stay in denial, the more debt you will accumulate, and the weaker your credit score will become, which leads us directly to the next step.

*Put down the spade*: As in, immediately stop digging yourself into a debt hole. If your credit card is your proverbial spade, then stop using it to make purchases immediately. If you are about to apply for a new loan, don't do it. The new debt will hurt the "new credit" component of your credit score and make you look like a young borrower instead of someone with a consistent credit history. This doesn't mean you should take drastic action like closing your accounts because you still want to maintain a lengthy credit history, but it means using your income to make purchases and payments instead of doing this with credit. Accumulating new debt while trying to pay off existing debts is like trying to wipe a floor clean with a muddy mop. It's fruitless and will take you backward instead of forward financially.

*Lists are a form of power*: You've checked your credit report, you've accepted the reality of your situation, and you have put a halt to getting any new forms of debt. Like how we recommended that you draw up a monthly budgeting plan to stick to as you pay off your debts, make a list of every single debt you owe, no matter how small. This debt inventory will help you see the big picture. This list should include your credit card debt, clothing accounts, accounts held in any store, student debt, car installments, money you owe to family or friends, and cell phone account payments. Seeing all of your debt in black and white can be scary, but it is absolutely necessary to decrease the balance you owe, which is the second-highest factor that is weighed when credit bureaus determine your credit score. This list will also help you determine what is good debt instead of bad debt. Good debt is that which positively contributes to your credit score and is an investment in yourself, like a mortgage payment or a car installment. Bad debt would be credit card debt, store credit accounts, or money you owe to family members because you are more likely to spend it fast, spend recklessly, or miss payments, and this will negatively impact your credit score.

*Consult an expert*: As much as taking the steps to get informed about your credit score will help you in countless ways, it's impossible for you to know every detail about the financial world. That's why financial experts exist. You likely also have a full-time job, maybe a family, or pets to take care of, and it can be difficult to keep track of every expense, especially if they are unforeseen expenses that spring up on you. Consulting an expert can contribute to your credit score because they will be able to advise you before you make a financial decision or make a big purchase. Hiring a financial advisor or a bookkeeper could take some pressure off of you and reign in your spending when an expert lays out how your debt will impact your life in the long term.

*Picture it*: Yes, you could interpret this as telling you to picture your life debt-free, and you should be doing that already. However, this step involves visualizing your debt by picturing what you owe and how long it will take to pay it off. Famous entrepreneur Robert Kiyosaki offers an excellent way to visualize your debt using a "Cashflow Quadrant" (Kiyosaki, 2020). Draw a line down the middle of a page and another line across the width of the page. Write the name of the debt in the upper left quadrant (e.g., "clothing account"). Move across to the upper right quadrant and write down how much you still owe on this debt (e.g., $1,000). Move down to the lower left quadrant and write down the minimum monthly amount you have to pay towards this debt (e.g., $50). Now divide the full amount you owe by the minimum monthly payment (e.g., $1,000 divided by $50). Write down the answer in the lower right quadrant and highlight or circle this number because this is the number of months it will take to pay off that entire debt (e.g., 20 months). Having a visual or even a vision board where you draw up all of your debts this way will put you on a path to reducing your remaining balance and improving your payment history, both of which contribute to your overall credit score.

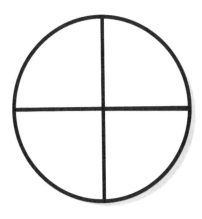

*Prioritize*: Now that you know exactly how much debt you owe and what you need to be paying towards, the next step is to choose which debts to pay off first and last. Use the numbers you highlighted or circled in your cashflow quadrants to determine which debt can be paid off quickly and make this your first priority. Starting with the debts that need fewer months to be paid off will increase your credit score by reducing your outstanding balance each month.

*Start a side hustle*: Having a debt to pay doesn't mean that you aren't allowed to have dreams, ambitions, or plans for growth. This next step involves finding some way to make an extra $100 to $200 a month. This extra income can come from places and things you come across daily. It could be the old furniture or appliances you have lying around in your garage, those seemingly useless infomercial kitchen gadgets you bought on the late-night shopping channel, or you could sell items on behalf of other people and take a cut of the profit. If you're good at it, you could also bake goods or cook food to sell as a side hustle. Becoming a delivery guy after your day job could also earn you some good extra income. Earning a bit of extra income will help you see the light at the end of the tunnel of debt because you are on your way to being able to pay back as much or more than you spent. This will help your debt-to-credit ratio, which will look positive to lenders and might raise or keep your credit score stable instead of dropping it.

*Don't do more than you have to*: You have prioritized your debts, and you are starting by paying off the debt that requires the least amount of time to be paid off in full. Now, pay the minimum required amount on your highest-priority debt. Next, take the extra $200 you've made and also pay it towards your highest priority debt. This means that you are not spending anything extra towards your highest-priority debt from your own pocket. Instead, you are using the extra money you earned to dissolve this debt faster. The feeling of relief you'll feel when you get to cross that first debt completely off your list will make your side hustle worth it. While you are taking care of your first priority debt, use your income to pay only the minimum monthly payments on the rest of your debts. Your credit score will only benefit from paying off your debts faster and getting out of the red into the black because credit bureaus are not looking at large lump sum payments of debts. They are looking for consistency and solid credit habits.

*Keep it moving*: Now you start having to juggle a few balls. Don't get complacent after paying off your first debt. Start paying your second highest priority debt by paying the minimum monthly payment for this debt, and then take the amount you were paying on your first debt and use it to pay off a bit extra on the second debt. Most importantly, continue your side hustle and pay the minimum payment on all your other debts. Repeat this process until you have paid off all of your debts.

*Invest in yourself*: Once you've made the final payment on your last priority debt, take a moment to celebrate, then take this monthly amount and continue to pay it into an investment. You will have finally reached a point where you are growing your income instead of seeing it disappear towards debt every month. It is very likely that the five components of your credit score would have improved by this point because your payment history would be consistent as you were making payments every month; the balance you owe on your debts would be close to zero besides a revolving credit card that you kept open; your credit history is being maintained at a steady pace; you should have a healthy mix of credit because you would have eliminated bad credit and you can now pay back more than you are spending; and finally, you would have stopped accumulating new credit when you started the process, so you should not look suspicious to lenders you want to apply to for future credit.

## ACTION STEPS

Based on the 10 steps described above, have a brain-storming session either on your own or with your partner or spouse to put together your own plan of attack for repairing your credit score that suits your personal financial situation and lifestyle and is relative to your current credit score. In the next chapter, we'll go over exactly what the Section 609 Dispute Letter is, how it works, and how you can use it to increase or repair your credit score.

# THE 609 DISPUTE LETTER AND HOW IT COULD SAVE YOUR FINANCIAL SKIN

*Let us never negotiate out of fear. But let us never fear to negotiate.* –John F. Kennedy

## WHAT IS A SECTION 609 DISPUTE LETTER?

In previous chapters, you've learned how important it is to start your credit repair journey by checking your credit report for any potential errors. You can attempt to dispute these mistakes using a "609 dispute letter". This letter is based on Section 609 of the Fair Credit Reporting Act (FCRA). The Section gives credit reporting agencies the responsibility or legal obligation to disclose information they used to calculate your credit score to prove that it is correct if you dispute this information. Credit bureaus and credit reporting agencies are legally required to verify disputed information in a credit report for the purposes of protecting the consumer. 609 dispute letters can be used as a tool to repair your credit because they are an official written request that you send to a bureau to remove incorrect information from your credit report.

A 609 dispute letter can be a critical step in improving your credit score because having errors removed from your credit report can greatly increase your credit score. The information in your credit report has to be as accurate as possible because it is used by lenders to decide whether or not to accept your credit applications. Having your credit applications continuously rejected by lenders because of incorrect information on a report you are not responsible for drafting is unfair to you as a consumer. This is the loophole that section 609 protects you from.

Generally, credit agencies or bureaus must respond to a 609 letter within 30 to 45 days with proof that they have accurately verified the information in your report. If the information is verified as true, then it stays on your report. If they don't respond to the letter, they will be in breach of the FCRA, and you can demand that the information be removed from your report. If they can't verify the information, then they will have to remove the information you disputed. Therefore, if you have a low credit score, you have nothing to lose by disputing any negative information on your credit report. It could only help your credit score or keep it where it currently is.

## WHAT DO YOU USE DISPUTE LETTERS FOR?

The 609 dispute letter is the first part of filing an actual dispute to remove errors in your credit report. The 609 letter is a request for information and a request to verify that information. Therefore, if you check your credit report and find that your personal or identifying information is incorrect or outdated, or there are duplicate or incorrect transactions on your report, or the report shows accounts you have already paid as outstanding or delinquent, or the report shows that you have made late payments when you know you have paid your accounts on time, you have grounds to send through a 609 letter. Any credit information that the credit agency can't verify must be deleted from your credit report by the reporting agency. Studies show that one in five people has errors on their credit reports (Sandberg, 2022).

When you check your credit report, identify the incorrect information you want to dispute in the 609 letters. Next, use the credit bureau's online form or submit your own 609 letters to officially file a dispute that states the information you want to dispute. The credit bureau will take 30 to 45 days to investigate your claim. Within five working days, you will be informed if your dispute was either successful and the mistakes will be removed from your credit report, or your dispute has been rejected. You can choose to consult a credit lawyer and take the dispute further even after it's been rejected.

This credit repair method is often successful in improving people's credit scores. However, the 609 dispute letter can't be used to avoid paying back the credit you still owe by removing these items from your credit report. Accurate, correct, and up-to-date credit information cannot be removed from your credit report with a 609 letter.

## HOW DO YOU WRITE A DISPUTE LETTER?

A 609 letter is a legal document, so you must keep it simple and straight to the point. It's not a motivational letter to ask a credit bureau to forgive your bad credit history, and it's not a letter of demand where you are demanding the allegedly incorrect information to be removed. The letter must be worded to prompt the bureau or agency to investigate and verify the information you're questioning. It's essential that you address your 609 letter to the correct entity. It must be addressed to one of the three main credit bureaus: Experian, Equifax, or TransUnion. The letter must specify exactly which items on your credit report you want to dispute and the details of these items. Your letter must be clear and concise without any ambiguity about what is actually being disputed.

## WHAT TO INCLUDE IN YOUR DISPUTE LETTER

The fact that 609 letters are used so often as a reliable credit repair strategy over the years, the information you need to include in them has become standardized, aside from the details of the actual items you want to dispute. Before you write your letter, collect all the documents that are relevant to your dispute and file them somewhere in date order. These documents include the credit report you are disputing and the documents that you have to prove that the information is incorrect (e.g., a proof of payment screenshot to prove that you paid your car installment if the report says you didn't).

Next, make sure you have the following information at hand to include in your letter:

- Proof of your identity, which could be your social security number, a copy of your driver's license, a utility bill, or your ID document.
- Your personal information, like your full name, phone number, and home address.
- The credit report that contains the information you are disputing with this information is highlighted or circled.
- Details about the credit information you are disputing. These must correspond to the items you have highlighted on your credit report.
- A request to have this incorrect information removed if it can't be verified by the credit bureau within 30 days.
- The account number you have with the credit bureau you are sending the letter to.
- A reference to Section 609 of the FCRA as the basis for filing your dispute. You should mention your right to request and receive the information and documents used to create your credit report.
- A list of the documents you have enclosed or attached to the letter and annexures.
- Your official signature.

Make copies of all of your documents and your 609 letters to keep a good record of your disputes because properly organizing your information will help if you have to take the dispute further and consult a credit lawyer. The final step is to send your letter to the relevant credit bureau by certified mail, and make sure to ask the post office for a return receipt to track the delivery of the letter to the bureau. The receipt is proof that the letter was delivered.

## AN EXAMPLE OF A DISPUTE LETTER

A 609 letter is simple enough to draft, and you definitely won't need to pay a company to do this for you. Let's look at an example of a simple 609 letter template that you can use as a foundation for your letter (Millstein, 2021).

*[Your Name]*

*[Your Address]*

*[Your Phone Number]*

*Your Bureau Account Number*

*Name of Credit Company/Point Person*

*Relevant Department*

*Address of Credit Reporting Agency*

*Date*

*Dear Sir or Madam,*

*I am writing to exercise my right to dispute the following items on my file. I have made note of these items on the attached copy of the report I have received from your agency. You will also find attached copies of documents that prove my identity, birth date, SSN, and address.*

*As is stated in the Fair Credit Reporting Act (FCRA), Section 609:*

*[In this section, include a relevant quote based on which area you are trying to dispute. You can look on the Federal Trade Commission's website for the official document with exact verbiage. Make sure you note which sub-section you are quoting from.]*

*See Attached: [List attached documentation here.]*

*The items I wish to dispute are as follows:*

*[Include as many relevant items as you have, up to 20, including the account name and number as listed on your credit report.]*

*These are [incorrect, inaccurate, unverified] due to the lack of validation by numerous parties that is required by Section 609. I have attached copies of relevant documentation.*

*I would appreciate your assistance in investigating this matter within the next 30 days. As required by the FCRA, if you fail to do so, all aforementioned information/disputed items must be deleted from the report.*

*SINCERELY,*

*[Your signature]*

*[Your name]*

*SEE ATTACHED: [List attached documentation here.]*

## ACTION STEPS

Practice writing your own 609 dispute letter that deals with your specific credit situation. We will also look at a few more letter template options in Chapter 15 for you to choose from and apply to your circumstances. In the next chapter, we'll unpack what credit inquiries are, how they impact your credit score, and the process involved in removing hard inquiries from your report.

# REVIEW PAGE

# My Readers Trust Your Opinion... Can You Help?

*"People appreciate and never forget that helping hand especially when times are tough."* — *Catherine Pulsifer*

Cast your mind back to the section where we discussed the things lawyers and lenders won't tell you about raising bad credit. There's a reason you picked up this book – and that's because you needed an outside eye on the situation – someone who doesn't have a vested interest or a service to sell you.

That's what most of us are looking for when we're searching for advice on financial matters – an impartial point of view whose opinion we can trust. That's why book reviews are so important. You don't necessarily trust the sales pitch of someone who's going to make money from the book – the bookseller, the publisher, the author... The opinions you really want to hear come from other readers – ordinary people like you who have implemented the advice they've read.

You have the chance to provide that information to other people in your position – and it will take just a few minutes of your time.

**By leaving a review of this book on Amazon, you can let other readers know how useful you found it, and what they can expect from reading it.**

It's only by reading the honest opinions of other people that new readers will know whether this is the resource they're looking for. They don't trust lawyers or lenders; they don't trust authors or publishers... They trust *you*. So if you could spend a minute leaving your opinion on Amazon, you can help point other people in the direction of the guidance they're looking for.

Thank you so much for your support. I want to assist as many people as I can – but I'm going to need your help to get there.

# HOW TO REMOVE HARD INQUIRIES FROM YOUR CREDIT REPORT

## WHAT ARE INQUIRIES?

An inquiry is the technical financial term for when your credit report is requested. Whenever you, a potential creditor, a potential employer, an insurance company, or a bank requests your credit report from a credit bureau or a credit reporting agency, it triggers an inquiry to be recorded on your credit report. Anyone accessing your credit report has to have the authority to do so, and you usually give them this authority to do a credit check when you submit a credit application form. The lender will want to check your credit history and score to decide whether or not to approve your credit application. Inquiries impact your credit score, and we'll get to the explanation of how this happens, but first, let's distinguish between the different types of inquiries and which of these can actually hurt your credit score.

'Soft' inquiries are noted on your credit report when you request your own credit report. Soft inquiries are also when an authorized person checks your credit for a reason that doesn't involve lending you money or credit. This can be a telemarketing company that wants to offer you a vacation package, an inquiry by your future employer, or a car insurance company that offers you a good premium if you have a good credit score. Soft inquiries appear on your credit report, but they do not affect your credit score at all because they have nothing to do with the risk you pose to a creditor.

"Hard" inquiries are recorded on your credit report when you apply for a new form of credit, and the creditor requests your credit report in connection with this application. Lenders will usually run credit checks when you apply for a credit card, a normal loan, a business loan, car financing, or a mortgage. They are directly related to the lender's wanting to find out how risky it would be to lend you money. These types of inquiries can stay on your credit report for up to two years, and they do affect your credit score for at least one year before bureaus and reporting agencies eventually ignore them.

## HOW DO HARD INQUIRIES IMPACT YOUR CREDIT?

Hard inquiries have an impact on the "new credit" component of your credit score. This component only makes up 10% of the factors that are weighed up to generate your credit score, but they are worth discussing to learn how to avoid having continuous hard inquiries appear on your credit report and staying there for years. The inquiries can lower your credit score because they are a direct result of how many times you apply for new credit. Applying for new credit within a short space of time makes you look like an inexperienced borrower and raises red flags with lenders. They will get the impression that you are either taking on new credit to pay off old debt or that the risk of your missing payments is high because you are over-committing yourself financially.

When assessing the new credit aspect of your credit score, credit bureaus, and credit reporting agencies will look at how long ago and how many times you've applied for new credit. If you've applied many times recently, your credit score could drop by a few points. The way the new credit component is balanced against the other four components will be unique for everyone because every person has a different credit file. Having a short credit history can also increase the impact of hard inquiries on your credit score because it relates to your consistency and experience as a debtor. Credit bureaus will probably lower the score of someone with many hard inquiries and short credit history because it shows that they might not be able to manage too much new credit.

It is agreed across the credit industry that the impact of hard inquiries on your credit score is relatively low as compared to other factors like missing payments or owing a large balance on your credit card. However, there are ways to lessen the impact of hard inquiries on your credit score before they even start accumulating. As per the definition of a hard inquiry, every time you apply for a new credit card or other loans, a hard inquiry could be triggered and recorded on your credit report. This means that if you apply for a new credit card in March, an auto loan in May, and a new cell phone contract in July, this will trigger three separate hard inquiries on your credit report because each credit provider will run their own credit check on your history. However, you can avoid this with a concept called "rate shopping" (Capital One, 2021). This means that you have to research the types of credit you need and think you should apply for, and then submit all these applications at once within a period of 30 to 45 days instead of spacing them out. This will result in only one collective hard inquiry being recorded on your credit report for the credit checks run within this time frame. Fewer hard inquiries will reduce the negative impact on your credit score. Note that rate shopping is usually effective when applying for car financing, mortgages, and student loans, so try to submit your applications for these types of credit all at once.

## HOW TO REMOVE HARD INQUIRIES FROM YOUR CREDIT SCORE

Experts note that hard inquiries usually only drop your score by about 5–10 points, but this could mean the difference between a fair and a good credit score, depending on your personal circumstances (Black, 2021). Therefore, it's worth having these hard inquiries removed if you can because you have nothing to lose.

As per the common thread throughout the credit repair methods we have gone through so far, the first step is to check your credit report. Request it for free from any of the major credit bureaus or credit reporting agencies. Review your report and first check for any unauthorized hard inquiries. These could be in the form of loans you know you never applied for or company names you don't recognize. Use a 609 dispute letter to dispute the accuracy of these hard inquiries and have the bureau or reporting agency remove them from your report. Remember that authentic and correct hard inquiries will not be removed from your report, so make sure that you know the inquiry is incorrect before disputing it. Ensure you send your 609 dispute letter to the correct credit reporting authority. The agency or bureau you contact for the dispute must be the same one that gave you that credit report or credit score.

If you believe that your identity or credit information has been fraudulently accessed, you can report this to law enforcement and place a freeze over your credit reports that prevents anyone from accessing them for a certain period of time.

ACTION STEPS

Request your credit report and check it thoroughly for any recent hard inquiries that have been recorded. Note down any inquiries you don't recognize or think might be fraudulent. Consider whether a 5–10 point decrease would make a major difference to your credit score. If it would, start the process of having them removed by filing a dispute with the relevant credit bureau or credit reporting agency that gave you the copy of your report. In the next chapter, we'll look at what late payments are, their impact on your credit score, and the process involved in removing them from your credit report.

# HOW TO MAKE LATE PAYMENTS DISAPPEAR FROM YOUR CREDIT HISTORY

## WHAT COUNTS AS A LATE PAYMENT?

The entire credit system, and especially the credit scoring system, is based on your ability as a debtor to pay back the required amount and pay it back on time. This is why the payment history component that contributes to your credit score weighs the heaviest. Your payment history tells lenders how reliable you are as a borrower and if you are consistent in paying off your debts over time. Late payments, or 'defaults' are directly related to the payment history of your credit score. A late payment is a payment made 30 or more days after the payment was initially due. For example, if you have to pay $100 towards your credit card bill on or before August 31 and you pay it on October 31, it is a late payment.

Paying $50 of that $100 on or before August 31 won't prevent your payment from being recorded as late if you don't pay the remaining $50 within 30 days of August 31. Late payments will only appear on your credit report if they are 30 or more days late. Therefore, in our example, if you paid $50 on August 31 and the other $50 on September 15, this will not be recorded as a late payment. Paying $50 on August 31 and the other $50 on October 31 makes the entire payment of $100 a late payment.

You might not have the police show up at your door because of late payments, but many people fail to understand the significance of late payments. Items like late payments can remain on your credit report for about seven years, so when you skip a payment thinking it's no big deal, there is actually a seven-year storm brewing behind the scenes that could completely ruin you financially unless you take the right action immediately.

## HOW DO LATE PAYMENTS AFFECT YOUR SCORE?

Statistics show that late payments can decrease your credit score by up to 100 points (O'shea, 2022). This is because making payments on time and in full are the most important requirements for generating a good credit score. Pay your debts on time to avoid your accounts being regarded as delinquent on your credit report, which is an account that has either been paid more than 30 days late or has not been paid at all. As much as there are four other relevant factors used to calculate your credit score (balance owed, length of your credit history, credit mix, and new credit), your payment history and ability to make payments on time make the biggest difference to your credit score. Losing 100 points on your score can mean the difference between being able to buy a house, finance a car, or get approved for a student loan to further your career. Most creditors will pay more attention to late payments on your report than any other negative items, because missing payments directly translates into you being a high-risk or irresponsible borrower.

Credit bureaus, credit reporting agencies, and lenders are not by your side on a daily basis to see exactly how you manage your finances, which is why your credit report and credit score give them a holistic view of what kind of debtor you are likely to be when they measure your credit history against their scoring system. Therefore, a creditor might not care if you struggled to make your payments for a five-month period but then bounced back to making consistent payments for the next three years. The bottom line is that late payments are a serious blemish on your credit report and they are poisonous to the health of your credit score.

## HOW TO DELETE LATE PAYMENTS FROM YOUR CREDIT REPORT

As always, when starting out a credit repair method, start by requesting your credit report. It is recommended that you check your credit report at all three of the major credit bureaus because late payments can have such a significant influence on your credit score. If you have been skipping payments or letting payments run late for months on end, chances are that you are struggling to keep a good record of your payments and how much you owe. Having a copy of your credit report will help you see where you went wrong at a glance. If you have been having difficulty coming to grips with your bad credit situation and you're hesitant about seeing your entire credit history, just think about the difference that 100 points to your credit score could make to your quality of life.

Look through your credit report and check for any payments that have been recorded as late. When checking your report for late payments, first look for late payments that you think might be errors in the debt amount, in the account number, contain duplicate payments or accounts, or are older than seven years. Cross-check any late payments you find in your report against the payment records you might have to confirm if they are true or not. If you find any late payments that you are fairly certain could be errors, then you have reasonable grounds to try to have these late payments removed from your credit report using a 609 dispute letter. Before you start the ball rolling to remove them using the dispute process, make sure you double-check them and confirm that they are incorrect because you will not be able to dispute valid late payments to erase them. The late payments you try to dispute have to be actual errors. You can send your 609 dispute letter either to the creditor first to verify the accuracy of the late payment and let them inform the credit bureau or credit reporting agency to have it removed from your credit report. You can also send your 609 letter directly to the bureau or reporting agency that gave you the credit report. The creditor, agency, or bureau will investigate the late payment and confirm that it's true within 30 days or remove it after 30 days if it can't be verified as accurate.

If you know that the late payments on your credit report are accurate or if you file a dispute and the bureau or reporting agency verifies that it is true, you still have two more options to try and get the late payments removed from your credit report. The first of these options is to write a "goodwill letter" to the creditor/s where you missed your payments. This method is particularly helpful if it's the first time you have missed a payment, your credit history and score are generally good, and you usually make your payments on time. You can use this letter to build your case to prove that you are usually a consistent and reliable debtor. An explanation of why you could not make those payments on time must be included in the letter, and you must ask for the creditor's forgiveness and understanding. It's worth including any steps you have taken to ensure you never miss another payment. This sounds like a simple option, but it is not guaranteed success because creditors are legally required to report correct information about your payment history to reflect on your credit report. It might be worth a try to appeal to the creditor's good nature if you can prove your creditworthiness.

The other option is to write the creditor a "pay-for-delete" letter. Pay-for-delete is basically a trade-off you make with the debt collector where the late payment is removed from your account once you settle the account and pay the amount you owe. This sounds like a good option to consider if a debt collection agent has been hunting you down and constantly calling you to ask you to make your late payments. However, the problem of creditors being legally required to report your late payments to bureaus and reporting agencies is growing. There is even less guarantee that this method will work than the goodwill letter because you are dealing with the debt collection agency as the middleman between you and the creditor. We'll look at examples of pay-for-delete letters in more detail in Chapter 15. Given the impact that late payments have on your credit score and the difficulty in removing them, it seems logical to focus on how to avoid late payments altogether.

## HOW TO AVOID LATE PAYMENTS

Life happens, expensive emergencies suddenly pop up, and sometimes you cannot stretch your income as far as it needs to go to pay all of your bills on time or in full. You're trying your best to stay afloat in an unpredictable economy while doing everything you can to give yourself and your family a consistently higher quality of life. It's always good to be kind to yourself, especially given the burden that financial stress can put on your mental health. Since you are already on the path to making changes to your financial health and turning it into financial wealth, let's look at a few ways to avoid late payments from even making their way to your credit report.

It might sound obvious, but paying your bills on time is the best way to avoid late payments. If you are fairly financially stable, set up automatic payments via your banking app to ensure that the amounts you owe automatically go off your account before their due date. Stagger these automatic payment dates around the day you get paid so that your account is replenished with your income after the payments go off.

If you have missed a payment and know it's going to be at least another 30 days before you can afford to pay it, bite the bullet and pay it late. It's a hard pill to swallow, but sometimes skipping payments is unavoidable. However, try to bring the account back into its current status as soon as possible because paying the full amount 30 days late is better for your credit score than paying it 60 days late, and so on. The longer you let the amount sit unpaid, the worse it is for your credit score and the sooner your account will be declared delinquent.

Once your missed payment hits the 30-day mark, it will be deemed a late payment. Try your best to contact your creditor before the late payment gets added to your credit report. You might be able to work out a payment plan, or the creditor might appreciate your courtesy and give you a chance to make the missing payments over the next few weeks before adding them to your credit report. Contacting the creditor cannot guarantee you a chance of avoiding having a late payment reflected on your credit report. Your final option would be to consult with a credit repair expert to try and have the late payments removed from your credit report.

ACTION STEPS

Check your credit report for any late payments, and verify if they are correct or erroneous. Assess your situation to determine the best route to take to have them removed. Consider if you are certain that the late payments are errors or if you will have to try writing a goodwill letter. Next, brainstorm the best strategy that will help you avoid making your payments late. Charge-offs are the focus of the next chapter, and we'll look at how to go about having them removed from your credit report.

# MAKE COLLECTIONS AND CHARGE-OFFS VANISH INTO THIN AIR

*Worry is the interest paid by those who borrow trouble.* –
George Washington

## WHAT IS A CHARGE-OFF?

Late payments are definitely one of the worst negative or derogatory marks to have on your credit report, but it can get one level worse if a charge-off appears on your credit report. A payment that is made 30 or more days after it is due is officially regarded as a late payment, but this refers to a single payment on one account or many different accounts. A charge-off means that the creditor has decided to write off your entire account because it has not been paid. The account will be regarded as a delinquent account, and the lender will write it off as a charge-off if the monthly payments have not been made for between 120 and 180 days. The creditor writes your delinquent off as a financial loss they are willing to absorb. This means that there can be no future charges to this account and it is closed on the creditor's end.

Don't celebrate just yet because you still have to pay the debt because, besides the account appearing as a charge-off on your credit report, the lender will probably sell the account to a debt collection agency to hound you until they get you to pay the remaining balance. Before and after the creditor declares your account as a charge-off, they will probably send you official letters to remind you to pay them to show that they tried everything they could to get you to pay. Debt collection agencies will continue this practice when they buy the delinquent account from the creditor. If you fail to pay the debt collection agency the amount you owe, they can sue you for the amount, and you can either appear in court and discuss some kind of payment plan with the agency by force of the law or, if you don't appear, the agency can get a default judgment against you. This kind of judgment would show up on your credit report and drag your score right down.

Like with late payments, partial payments that are less than the required monthly minimum can still lead to your account being charged off. Not paying enough into your account each month results in the detection of late payments, and multiple late payments eventually lead to a delinquent account that is charged off. Essentially, your accounts need to be paid in full (meaning at least the monthly minimum payment) and on time for you to dodge charge-offs.

Charge-offs are extremely bad for your credit score because they show that you are incapable of managing your credit and finances in general. After all, having a charge-off on your report means you have missed payments on an account for at least four to six months. You will show up as extremely high-risk to new creditors, and it will not only drop your credit score but make you unlikely to be successful in any new credit applications. Remember that creditors don't know you personally and make decisions using the numbers and information on your credit report, which is used to calculate your credit score. Charge-offs can bring down your credit score because they stay on your report for at least seven years from the date of the first late payment on the account. Another superpower of charge-offs is that one delinquent account can appear twice on your credit report. If a creditor has written the account off as delinquent and sold it to a debt collection agency, this counts as one negative mark on your report. The charge-off now sitting with the debt collector while they try to get you to pay is a second negative mark that can appear on your credit report. Charge-offs can stay on your credit report even after you pay the debt collector in full, but their impact on your credit score wears off after seven years have passed. You definitely don't want to wait seven years to improve your credit score, and charge-offs directly affect your payment history and balance owed components of your credit score, so it's important to try and have them removed from your report.

## RESOLVING CHARGE-OFFS AND DEBT COLLECTIONS

Start by checking your credit reports with all three major credit bureaus for any charge-offs that have been recorded either by creditors or by debt collection agencies. If you believe that these charge-offs are errors, incorrect, or outdated, then you are entitled to start the dispute process by filing a dispute with the credit bureau or reporting agency that issued that credit report. Prepare your 609 dispute letter and list the charge-off items that you know to be errors on your report. As per the usual process, the credit bureau will receive your 609 dispute letter, investigate the charge-offs and either verify their accuracy or respond that they will be removed if they can't be verified. Remember, you can't use the 609 dispute letter or the dispute process to dispute charge-offs that are true, accurate, and up-to-date because credit companies are legally required to report correct information on your credit report.

Another option to remove charge-offs from your credit report is to directly contact your creditor. As we discussed with late payments, this method is not always reliable because the creditor is legally required to record accurate information about your credit history, even if this information shows you to be a bad debtor. You can write the creditor a letter to explain your situation, try to humanize the numbers in your credit report, and hopefully convince them to work out a payment plan with you to pay off the remaining balance in full or over a set time period. You can ask the creditor to 're-age' your account after you have paid the balance in full. This means asking the creditor to change the account's status from delinquent to current or active. This might cancel out the negative impact of the charge-off on your credit score with the positive of paying off the account, and it remains active. This is equivalent to a pay-for-delete request, so there's no guarantee that it will work, but if the only thing that happens is that the charge-off remains on your credit report, then there's no harm in trying.

The next option is to contact a trustworthy credit repair company to help you get your financial affairs in order. These companies will charge you a fee for consultations and for looking through your documents. It's very important to do some research before approaching these credit repair companies because some of them can be fraudsters trying to scam you out of your last few bucks that you are already trying to cling to by approaching them in the first place. A legal credit repair company might be a worthwhile option if you have exhausted all of the other options on your own and still can't get the charge-offs removed from your report.

The final and possibly the worst option is to simply wait for the charge-off's impact to wear off. This means either waiting seven years for the charge-off to become outdated in relation to your credit report, or waiting for the debt to expire as per the statute of limitations in your state. The waiting game is stressful, and the thought of spending three to seven years dodging debt collection agency calls is not the best future prospect, so try out all the other options before deciding to wait.

## ACTION STEPS

Check your credit reports with all the credit bureaus for any accounts that have gone into debt collection or charge-offs and select at least one option from the above to try and have the charge-off removed from your report. Next, we'll explore a few other negative marks that could appear on your credit report and the steps you need to take to remove them.

# HOW TO REMOVE OTHER ITEMS FROM YOUR CREDIT REPORT

*A man who pays his bills on time is soon forgotten.* –Oscar Wilde

The quote above is significant because it explains why good credit practices and financial habits will always be better for you than the opposite. If you make your payments in full and on time, you will breeze through most, if not all, credit applications and be granted access to credit that you know how to manage well. However, if you have a bad credit score or a history of inconsistent credit habits, you will raise red flags with any creditor you submit a loan application to.

## COMMON NEGATIVE ITEMS TO LOOK OUT FOR ON YOUR CREDIT REPORT

Negative items on your credit report can be any item that makes you look like an unreliable borrower, and that would drop your credit score. You should check your credit report at least once a year for any of the most common negative items found on credit reports, which are listed below.

*Bankruptcy*: Filing for bankruptcy means you are officially unable to pay any debts. Declaring bankruptcy involves a legal procedure, and you can make an agreement with the federal authorities to exchange an asset like your house as collateral to settle the debt you owe. Bankruptcy is the worst possible outcome for your credit lifespan because it means you have to start building credit from scratch and, depending on the type of bankruptcy you file for, it can stay on your credit report for between three to 10 years. Potential creditors will be very wary of your risk to them, and your credit score will reach record lows.

*Late payments*: These are payments that have not been paid for more than 30 days past their due date. Having a late payment on your credit report directly affects the payment history component of your credit score by indicating that you are not reliable enough to make your payments on time. These stay on your credit report for up to seven years and are one of the most common and also most influential negative marks on your report.

*Charge-offs*: This is a late payment that has still not been paid for between 120 and 180 days. The creditor writes off the delinquent account as a loss, and it's regarded as a charge-off on your credit report. The creditor will then either try to contact you in writing to get you to settle the account, or they will sell the written-off account to a debt collection agency who will try to contact you as well. Charge-offs stay on your credit report for up to seven years, and they are very difficult to remove. They directly affect the payment history and balance owed portions of your credit score.

*Collection*: A debt collection agency will do everything possible to recover the amount you owe on an account. Debt collection agencies buy off charged-off accounts from creditors for less than the balance that is owed, and they try to make a profit off of them by getting you to pay what you owe. They will use every means they can to contact you, including phone calls, messages, emails, and formal letters. The debt you owe the creditor will count as one negative mark on your report, and the same debt you owe that has been transferred to the debt collector will become a separate negative mark on your report. If you ignore a debt collector, it could be bad for your credit score because they have the right to take legal action against you to recover the debt you still owe.

*Civil claim*: This is a major blemish on your credit report because of the way the path of bad credit escalates from one missed payment to your account being declared delinquent to it becoming a charge-off to your creditor, from them selling off the account to a debt collector to the debt collector being unable to get you to pay, and eventually ends up in court as a civil claim against you for the amount you owe. A civil claim can result in a default judgment being made against you, where creditors are legally allowed to take your wages or property to recover the money you owe them. Your bank accounts can also be frozen if there is a claim against you. Having a civil claim on your credit report shows that you cannot manage your finances, especially your debts.

*Foreclosure*: Late mortgage payments can lead to a creditor taking ownership of your home to use the property to pay off the debt. It stays on your credit report for up to seven years, and it will lower the payment history aspect of your credit score to a large degree. A mortgage is seen as one of the most important credit types, and so the consequences of not being able to pay it are more serious than for other types of credit.

*Lien*: This is failure to state or federal taxes on your income or your home. Missing these payments allows the government (state or national government) to attach a tax lien to your assets. The assets that might become attached to a tax lien could be your properties or your bank accounts. If you still don't pay the taxes you owe after the lien is effective, the lien will stay on your credit report permanently or until you pay those taxes. A lien is terrible for your credit score because it's an indication that the government has had to step in because of your failure to manage your credit. This won't sit well with potential lenders.

*Repossession*: This is equivalent to foreclosure but for unsecured loans or loans that have not been secured with collateral like a house. For example, if you've bought a car using an auto loan and you miss payments, the car financing company has the right to repossess or take ownership of the car to make up for the balance you still owe. Your credit score will suffer because a repossession of any type will show up on your credit score.

*Settlement accepted*: This is one of the less negative marks. It occurs when you make a payment plan with a creditor and pay off at least some of the outstanding balance, and the creditor agrees to consider this as a full settlement of the account. It might indicate on your credit report that you have missed payments, but a fully paid account looks better than a delinquent account.

*Account in credit counseling*: Consulting an expert to help you manage a mountain of credit debt can lead your creditors to sympathize with you and agree to report to credit bureaus that you have tried to get help to pay off your debt. You will need to approach Consumer Credit Counseling Services to help you negotiate lower monthly payment plans with your creditors in order to get this mark to reflect on your credit report.

*Voluntary surrender*: This is when you give any collateral or property that you've used to secure a loan back to the creditor because you admit to them that you are unable to pay back the debt due to a financial crisis. You can surrender collateral like your car or your house, and give it back to the creditor as payment of your debt. This negative mark on your credit report shows that you are unable to manage your debts and makes you look unreliable to potential creditors.

*Unknown (X)*: An X on your credit report means that the credit bureau or credit reporting agency that generated the report cannot verify whether or not the account the X is next to has been paid by you. It could be that they couldn't contact the creditor or that the account records were not available to view. This might not bring your score down, but it can prevent it from increasing, so sending a query to your creditor is worthwhile.

*Inquiry*: This is when someone requests your credit report to run a credit check. A soft inquiry is when you, a potential employer, or a telemarketer pull your credit report and the request has nothing to do with lending you credit. This doesn't affect your credit score. A hard inquiry is triggered when you apply for a loan or credit, and the potential creditor requests your credit report. Every hard inquiry can decrease your credit score by up to 10 points because it counts against the new credit component of your credit score by showing that you are applying for new credit too often.

## WHAT ARE DEROGATORY MARKS?

These are negative items that are recorded and stay on your credit report for between seven and 10 years and suggest that you have a habit of not paying your debts in full and on time. The negative items above can all become derogatory marks if they find their way onto your credit report. These marks can either be added to your credit report by the credit bureau or reporting agency preparing the actual report, or your creditors might have reported them to the bureaus or reporting agencies.

Derogatory items bring your credit score down because they indicate either an inconsistent and unreliable payment history spotted with late payments and charge-offs; a large balance that is still owed; a short credit history; a bad and unmanageable credit mix; or that you are applying for new credit far too often. These factors make up your credit score, and a low credit score combined with a few derogatory marks can prevent your credit applications from being approved, or you might end up paying sky-high interest rates on the loans you do get.

The negative impact of a derogatory mark on your credit score is relative to the seriousness of bad credit behavior on your part. For example, one late payment over a 12-month period might not have as bad an impact on your credit score as the foreclosure of your home in the same time period. The seriousness of the derogatory mark relates to how high you should prioritize that debt in your life. In this example, your mortgage payment should be a higher priority payment than your cell phone account.

## HOW TO REMOVE NEGATIVE ITEMS FROM YOUR REPORT

The solutions for removing negative or derogatory marks from your credit report are similar to those we have discussed in previous chapters, and they can be applied to each type of negative mark described above.

First, request and check your credit report for any derogatory marks. Note down the marks that you are fairly sure might be inaccurate, erroneous, or outdated (i.e., older than seven years). Next, prepare your Section 609 dispute letter to dispute the alleged errors and force the entity that sent you the report to verify the information you are disputing. Your dispute will be investigated within 30 days of your filing. It will either be rejected because the information was verified, or the negative mark will be removed by the next time you request your report. You can't use the dispute process to try and dispute factual and accurate information because this has to stay on your credit report even if it's bad for your credit score. If the information you disputed is proven to be true, try a few other methods to get those derogatory marks off your credit report.

Try contacting your creditor directly using a goodwill letter to appeal to them by explaining the reasons or context of how you ended up in the situation that caused the derogatory mark. If this is unsuccessful, try to negotiate a pay-for-delete agreement with the creditor where you agree to settle the account you defaulted on in exchange for having it removed from your credit report. This might leave a negative mark on your account, but the account status will change from delinquent to current or active, which might help your credit score slightly. Your last option is to wait seven years until the derogatory marks either fall off your credit report or have a lower impact on your credit score.

ACTION STEPS

Review your credit report for any negative items that you want to remove to see if your credit score will improve without them. Try out the various methods explained above to have them cleared from your credit report. Now that we've covered how you can fix or build up your credit score, let's move on to how you can continue to maintain a strong and healthy credit score going forward to secure a better future for yourself and your loved ones.

# THE KEYS TO KEEPING YOUR CREDIT SCORE SAFE AND HEALTHY

*If you would know the value of money, go and try to borrow some.* –Benjamin Franklin

## TIPS FOR MAINTAINING A STRONG CREDIT SCORE

Checking your credit report and finding out your actual credit score is definitely a step in the right direction toward financial freedom. However, your financial responsibilities won't disappear after you've taken all the steps we've discussed to release yourself from the clutches of debt. If your credit score improves or is repaired because of your actions, that's great. But now you need to consider how you plan on maintaining a strong credit score. There are various tips you can implement into your monthly financial routine that will reduce your stress levels about making ends meet each month and even allow you to save and grow some of your income.

*Stay familiar with FICO*: Understanding the FICO scoring system is essential to figuring out the strategies you need to adapt to repair your credit. Your credit score ranges from between 300 and 850, and your creditworthiness is usually placed on the following score sliding scale: 300-579 is considered poor, 580-669 is considered fair, 670-739 is considered good, 740-799 is considered very good, and 800-850 is considered excellent. If your score is high, it means you are a reliable credit user, and you pay your bills on time. If it's low, it means that you cannot find a balance between spending and paying back credit and you are a high risk to any potential creditor. FICO considers your profile as a borrower of credit as one big pie, and the pieces of this pie are weighted by FICO as follows:

- 35% of the score is made up by considering your payment history, which is how consistent you are in paying your bills on time.
- 30% is made up of the amount you still owe to creditors.
- 15% is made up of the length of your credit history, and a long history is better than a short

one because it shows you have been responsible with credit in the past.

- 10% is made up of new credit you have recently taken or applied for, and this should be kept to a minimum because too much new credit makes you a high-risk borrower.
- 10% is made up of the types of credit you use or your credit mix, and this involves balancing major types of credit like mortgages with less consequential credit like cell phone accounts (US Bank, 2020).

Each factor is like a paintbrush used to color in the picture of you as a borrower. Write these numbers and factors down somewhere so that you can make sense of them when looking at your own credit score and your own credit history.

*Check your credit regularly*: If becoming familiar with how the FICO scoring system works is the door to entering the room of freedom from debt, then regularly checking your credit report is the key to this door. The three major credit bureaus all keep their own credit reports on your credit history, and you are entitled to receive your report from them for free. Looking at your report will help you see exactly why your credit score is the number it is and also find ways to improve it. Use online service providers like Credit Karma, Annual-

CreditReport.com, Credit Sesame, or Credit Wise to access your credit reports or request them directly from the three major credit bureaus, Experian, Trans-Union, and Equifax.

*Be certain when reporting credit report errors*: Filing a dispute to remove errors from your credit report using Section 609 of the FCRA can be extremely helpful in boosting your credit score because fewer negative items on your report mean you have a better reputation as a borrower and are a relatively low risk to potential lenders. When choosing errors to dispute, make sure these are actually errors because if the information is verified by the reporting agency or bureau, it will stay on your credit report even if it makes you look like a high-risk credit user. To be certain of errors, always have your own records of your financial transactions to cross-reference your credit report against. Look for errors relating to duplicate accounts, mistaken identity, unauthorized credit checks, outdated negative items, and incorrectly recorded missed payments.

*Pay your bills on time*: This is the golden rule of maintaining a good credit score. Your credit score tells potential lenders how likely you are to pay them back and helps them decide whether or not to take on the risk of lending you money or giving you credit. Paying your bills on time keeps all the components that make up your credit score balanced. Remember that one missed payment can stay on your credit report for up to seven years, so use automatic payments, a monthly budget, or diary entries scattered around the day you get paid to make sure you pay your bills on time every month.

*Continuously reduce your balance owed*: If paying your bills on time is the golden rule of keeping your credit score high, then paying them in full gets the silver medal in second place. This doesn't mean paying the entire amount you owe in one lump sum payment, because this is often impossible and the reason why the credit system even exists. It means at least making the minimum required payment each month. This keeps the interest you have to pay at a reasonable rate in the long term. Prioritize the debt with the highest interest rates as those you will pay off first, or choose the debt that will take the fewest months to pay off first. If you can afford to throw a few extra dollars at some debts each month, then do so. Paying less than the monthly minimum will lead to late payments that damage your credit score.

*Maintain a low debt-to-credit ratio*: This ratio measures how much credit you have used against how much credit you have available. Keep this at a rate of 30% or lower to be in the clear and maintain the payment history and owing balance aspects of your credit score at a good rate. Statistics indicate that people with excellent credit scores only use 7% of their credit limits (Muller, 2022).

*Think twice before opening new accounts*: Applying for new credit will negatively impact the new credit aspect of your credit score, and it will trigger hard inquiries to be recorded on your credit report. These can drop your credit score by up to 10 points. Multiple new credit applications sent out in a short space of time raise red flags for potential lenders that you are either taking credit to pay off existing loans or you are open to the risk of not being able to manage too many new credit accounts. Practice rate shopping and submit all of your new credit applications in the space of 30 days to consolidate the credit checks run by your potential creditors into one hard inquiry on your credit report.

*Don't close old credit accounts*: Closing an old credit card can increase your credit utilization ratio by decreasing your credit limit even if you spend the same amount as when you had the old credit card open. Keeping old credit cards open also lengthens your credit history, which is good for your credit score. Take stock of all of your credit cards and credit accounts and spread them out over your monthly budget to see where you can make use of them without having to close them. For example, use one credit card to pay for gas and the other to buy your groceries or top up your credit card with some of your income to only dip into your credit limit once your own spending money has run out.

*Consolidate credit cards if you have too many*: If you're finding it difficult to manage your spending on multiple credit cards and you find that the usage of your credit limit is going unchecked, then try to transfer all of your credit limit and your remaining balance onto one card and use it to pay off all of your monthly bills. This might help you reduce your outstanding debt balance faster than spreading it out across different cards. Contact your credit card service to ask if this is an option.

*Stick to a budgeting plan and live within your means*: This might be easier said than done, and it does require some serious lifestyle changes, but if you keep yourself motivated by seeing your total amount of debt decrease every month, then it's worth it in the long term. If you live in a two-income household, try to save one entire income and invest it while stretching the other income to pay for every bill. If you are a single person, try to keep the amount of your income used to pay for credit card debt at less than 10% each month. Create a monthly budget and be patient as you implement it to make positive changes to your credit history and credit score.

## ACTION STEPS

Select at least two of the tips to maintain a strong credit score from the above and write them down somewhere you are likely to look at every day. Make these your financial mantras or create a financial vision board where you promise yourself to stick by these tips. Change these tips to new ones every few months so that you can try different strategies to find what works best for you. Use this as motivation to pay off your debts and continue maintaining your credit. In the next chapter, we'll explore the different types of debt and how you should manage each as you work toward repairing your credit.

# MANAGING DIFFERENT TYPES OF DEBT

The total amount of household debt in the USA has reached $16.15 trillion, and market trends indicate that this number will not decrease in the near future (Federal Reserve Bank of New York, 2022). A good understanding of the different types of debt can help you manage your debt and maintain a good credit score by ensuring that the mix of the types of credit that you use is not unmanageable. Credit bureaus don't look at every debt as equal to the next, and they have different impacts on your credit score. In this chapter, we'll review the different types of debt and how you should properly manage each so that they don't end up managing you.

## SECURED DEBT

This is when the amount you are borrowing on credit is secured by an actual asset that is called collateral. The asset can be a house, a car, or an investment. For example, your mortgage bond will be secured by your house, so if you miss any mortgage payments, the bond company or bank that granted you the mortgage can take ownership of or seize the house as security for payment of the loan. A pro of secured debt is that it gives you access to higher loan amounts because the money you borrow is tied up in an asset, so the creditor is guaranteed to be repaid even if you miss payments. Another pro is that interest rates will be reasonable because there is a lower risk to the creditor if the loan is secured by collateral.

The cons of secured debt are that you can only spend the money borrowed on that specific collateral asset and on nothing else, and the risk to you is high as you could lose your house or car by missing a payment. The best way to manage secured debt is to make your minimum monthly payments on time every month and to plan ahead because these are usually large and life-altering expenses. If you fall behind on payments, communicate with the bank or creditor to try and prevent the worst-case scenario of losing your home or car.

## UNSECURED DEBT

A creditor will lend you money that is not secured by an asset if they believe they can rely on you to pay it back. Unlike secured debt, the value of uncensored debt is not linked to an asset. You will have access to unsecured credit like credit cards, personal loans, and student loans if you have a high credit score and a good track record of paying back your debts on time. The pros of unsecured debt are that your assets are protected from being taken away to pay for the debt if you miss payments; you don't even need to own any assets to access unsecured credit, and applications for unsecured credit are usually granted faster than secured credit.

The cons of unsecured credit are that you need a good credit score to get access to it. This means that your credit report must show that you are able to pay your bills within the allocated time. Because unsecured debt is not backed up by property, this translates into a higher risk to the lender than a secured loan. Therefore, you might end up paying a higher interest rate on an unsecured loan. Once again, the best way to manage unsecured debt is to be strict about making your payments on time.

## REVOLVING DEBT

This is where the creditor puts a cap or limit on the amount of credit you can spend. Credit cards give you access to revolving debt. Spending revolving credit means the amount you have left to spend decreases because there is a set credit limit. The limit replenishes when you pay the money back onto the credit card, and your monthly repayment amount depends on when you pay, how much you have used, how much credit you have left, and the interest rate set by the credit provider. The pro of revolving debt is that you can manage your spending within the credit limit or either decrease or increase the credit limit, depending on your spending habits.

The negative aspects of revolving credit are that interest rates can fluctuate depending on your credit score, and it is very easy to overspend, thinking you can max out your credit limit. The best way to manage revolving debt is to remember that the money you are using is not your own and you will have to pay it back, so do everything you can to control your spending.

Another foolproof way to manage your credit is to pay back everything you spent from the credit limit every month or at least the monthly minimum payment you owe each month not to get hit with a high amount of interest or create late payments.

## INSTALLMENT DEBT

Examples of installment debt are car loans, student loans, personal loans, and mortgages because they can be secured or unsecured. An installment debt is a form of revolving debt because you are given a set amount of money that you have to pay back over the loan term or time period set by your creditor. The pros of installment debt are that they allow you to make important life purchases over long periods of time instead of having to pay for everything immediately.

The cons of installment debt are that having too many different types can become unmanageable and overwhelming, and having a fair to poor credit score means that you are likely to be charged high-interest rates on the amount you have to pay back each month. The best way to manage installment debt is to, once again, pay the installment on time every month and pay the full installment. If you can improve your interest rate on an installment loan by refinancing it, then do so to pay it off quicker. It's also a good strategy to throw extra cash into these types of loans every year. For example, if you get paid a bonus check, put the money into your mortgage or towards your car to pay it off faster.

## CREDIT CARD DEBT

This is the best example of revolving debt because you are not required to pay back the full amount of your credit limit you have used at the end of the month. You only have to pay a minimum portion of it back each month. The interest rate you will pay on your credit card repayments is usually about 15%, and it depends on your credit score and how much the creditor trusts you to pay back the amount you use on the card. The best way to manage a credit card is to pay back the full amount you have used every month because allowing the credit to revolve and only paying the minimum amount snowballs the interest you have to pay. Credit card debt payments are not tax deductible, but they can impact your credit score if you miss payments or try to juggle too many different credit cards at once.

## MORTGAGE DEBT

These are secured installment debts repaid to the creditor over a predetermined time period with set installment amounts paid each month. Missing payments or allowing them to turn into late payments (not paying an installment for more than 30 days) can result in your home being repossessed by the creditor in what is known as foreclosure. Mortgage loans generally have an interest rate of between 3% and 7%. You have to pay the full installment on time every month to avoid having your home foreclosed on. Up to $1,000,000 of the mortgage loan interest you pay on your main family home is tax-deductible. A mortgage loan is great for your credit score because it adds to your credit mix and shows potential creditors that you are reliable because you have your financial priorities in order.

## AUTO LOANS

This is also a secured installment loan that is paid over a predetermined time period set by the creditor. The car you drive off the showroom floor after signing up for this loan is the collateral that will be repossessed by the creditor if you miss payments. The interest rate of a car loan depends on the term of the loan. For example, if you have five years to pay it back, the interest rate will be lower than if you sign up to pay it back over three years. These loans are not tax-deductible and have no tax implications. Your credit score will improve if you make your car installment payments on time, and it will contribute to increasing the rating on the payment history portion of your credit score.

## STUDENT LOANS

This is a type of installment credit that is not secured by any property. The amount of the monthly repayment and the loan term are usually different for each student. Financial institutions are sometimes lenient on students by offering interest rates that stay the same throughout the loan term, or they are flexible with the loan repayment amount charged each month. The loan term is usually 10 years to give the student enough time to finish their studies and start working to earn money to repay the loan. Some credit providers or companies allow borrowers to work for them for several years or use their income to repay the loan. Up to $2,500 of interest paid on a student loan is tax-deductible if their gross income is under $80,000. Student loans contribute positively to the length of your credit history and to your payment history if you are able to make your payments on time each month.

MEDICAL DEBT

This credit is provided to you by a healthcare provider like a medical aid scheme, and they usually expect you to pay back the full amount owed when it's due. However, the financial departments of healthcare providers or hospitals can sometimes allow you to negotiate a payment plan to pay back your medical bills. If medical expenses make up more than 7.5% of your gross monthly income, they are tax-deductible if they form part of the permitted medical expenses like consultations with doctors, psychiatrists, dentists, chiropractors, and chronic medication like insulin.

The CFPB and the three main credit bureaus announced changes to the impact that medical debt will have on your credit score. From July 1, 2022, medical debt that has not been paid off will not be included in your credit report. Unpaid medical debt will only appear on your credit report after it has been left unpaid for a full year. From the first half of the year 2023, an unpaid medical debt of less than $500 will not appear on your credit report. These changes are significant because your credit score can improve if your medical debt meets the requirements not to be included in your credit report.

ACTION STEPS

Make a list of the current debts you have and categorize them by the type of credit they are made up of. Write out how your debt is allocated and use this to help you plan out the best repayment strategy that will not lead you to pay a high-interest rate. In the next chapter, we'll provide you with various templates to use when writing a 609 dispute letters and other types of correspondence with the purpose of repairing your credit score.

# THE MOST EFFECTIVE TEMPLATES FOR QUICKLY WRITING 609 LETTERS

*If you want to be successful, find someone who has achieved the results you want and copy what they do and you'll achieve the same results.* –Tony Robbins

## GENERAL TEMPLATES FOR 609 DISPUTE LETTERS

Below are a few examples you can use to word your 609 dispute letter to dispute any inaccurate, erroneous, or outdated information on your credit report to have this information removed and hopefully increase your credit score. Fill in your information in the relevant spaces. Submit the letter to the credit bureau or credit reporting agency that gave you the credit report you are disputing. Remember that the information you dispute must actually be incorrect, or the information will be verified and remain on your credit report.

### *609 Dispute Letter Template #1*

*[Your Name]*

*[Street Address]*

*[City, State Zip]*

*[Phone Number]*

*[Email]*

*[Date]*

SUBJECT: *Section 609 of the Fair Credit Reporting Act*

TO WHOM IT MAY CONCERN,

*I am pursuing my right to request information about item(s) listed on my credit report through the Fair Credit Reporting Act, Section 609.*

*[Give account names and numbers.]*

Based on section 609, I am exercising my right to see the original source of information that contains the contract with my signature.

I've included these documents to verify my identity:

Birth certificate

Social security card

Passport

Driver's license

W-2

Cell phone bill

You can also find an attached copy of my credit report with the portion that needs verification circled.

[If you have a lawyer, include this.] I have legal representation. Here is my lawyer's contact information: [lawyer name, address, phone number].

The information should be removed from my credit report in the next 30 days if you cannot verify the original contract with a signature.

SINCERELY,

[Signature]

[Full Name]

(Black, 2022).

### 609 Dispute Letter Template #2

[Your Name]

[Your Address]

[Your Phone Number]

[Your Account Number]


[NAME OF CREDIT COMPANY/POINT Person[

[Relevant Department[

[Address of Credit Company]


Date


DEAR [NAME of credit reporting agency],


I AM WRITING to exercise my right to question the validity of the debt your agency claims I owe, pursuant to the Fair Credit Reporting Act (FCRA).

As stated in Section 609 of the FCRA, (2) (E): A consumer reporting agency is not required to remove accurate derogatory information from a consumer's file unless the information is outdated under Section 609 or cannot be verified.

As is my right, I am requesting verification of the following items:

[List any/all items you're looking to dispute, including the account name(s) and number(s) as listed on your credit report]

Additionally, I have highlighted these items on the attached copy of the credit report I received.

I request that all future correspondence be done through the mail or email. As stated in the FCRA, you are required to respond to my dispute within 30 days of receipt of this letter. If you fail to offer a response, all disputed information must be deleted.

Thank you for your prompt attention to this matter.


SINCERELY

[Your signature]

[Your name]

.  .  .

*SEE ATTACHED: [List attached documents here.]*

*[Attach copies of proof of identity like your name, birth date, social security number, and current mailing address, along with a copy of your credit report with relevant items high-lighted]*

(Millstein, 2021).

### 609 Dispute Follow-Up Letter Template

Use this letter if the credit bureau or reporting agency has not responded to your initial dispute letter and more than 30 days have passed.

*[Your Name]*

*[Your Address]*

*[Your Phone Number]*

*[Your Account Number]*


*[NAME OF CREDIT COMPANY/POINT Person[*

*[Relevant Department[*

*[Address of Credit Company]*


*Date*

. . .

DEAR SIR OR MADAM,

MY NAME IS [YOUR NAME], and I reached out to you several weeks ago regarding my credit report. This letter is to notify you that you have not responded to my initial letter, dated [insert date]. I have restated the terms of my dispute below for your convenience.

[Insert information from your first letter about disputed items. Include disputed account names and numbers as listed on your credit report.]

Section 609 of the Fair Credit Reporting Act (FCRA) states that you must investigate my dispute within 30 calendar days from my initial letter. As you have failed to do so, I kindly request that you remove the aforementioned items from my credit report.

Any further comments or questions can be directed to my legal representative, [insert name], who can be reached at [insert phone number].

SINCERELY,

[Your signature]

[Your name]

. . .

*SEE ATTACHED: [List all attached documentation here, including copies of your credit report, proof of identity, proof of current mailing address, etc.]*

(Millstein, 2021).

## DEBT VALIDATION LETTER TEMPLATE

This letter allows you to request that a debt collection agency that has contacted you must provide you with proof to verify the debt you allegedly owe to them. You have 30 days from the first time the debt collector contacts you to give the information needed for this letter. The template below sets out the information you should ask the debt collector to provide, which will change depending on your specific circumstances.

*CREDITOR/DEBT Collector Declaration*

*Please provide all the following information and submit the appropriate forms and paperwork within 30 days from the date of your receipt of this debt validation request.*

*NAME AND ADDRESS of Alleged Creditor:*

*Name on File of Alleged Debtor:*

*Alleged Account Number:*

*Address on File for Alleged Debtor:*

*Amount of debt:*

*Date that this debt became payable:*

*Date of original charge off or delinquency:*

*Was this debt assigned to a debt collector or purchased?*

*Amount paid if the debt was purchased:*

*Commission for debt collector if collection efforts are successful:*

*Please attach a copy of the agreement with your client that grants (Collection Agency Name) the authority to collect this alleged debt.*

*Also, please attach a copy of any signed agreement the debtor has made with the debt collector or other verifiable proof the debtor has a contractual obligation to pay the debt collector.*

*Please attach a copy of any agreement that bears the debtor's signature, wherein they agreed to pay the creditor.*

*Please attach copies of all statements while this account was open.*

*Have any insurance claims been made by any creditor regarding this account?*

*YES or NO (circle one)*

*HAVE any judgments been obtained by any creditor regarding this account?*

*YES or NO (circle one)*

*PLEASE PROVIDE the name and address of the bonding agent for {Name Of Debt Collector}, in case legal action becomes necessary:*

*AUTHORIZED SIGNATURE For Creditor*

*Date*

. . .

*You must return this completed form along with copies of all requested information, assignments, or other transfer agreements, which would establish your right to collect this alleged debt within 30 days from the date of this letter.*

*Your claim cannot and WILL NOT be considered if any portion of this form is not completed and returned with copies of all requested documents. This is a request for debt validation made pursuant to the FDCPA. Please allow 30 days for processing after I receive this information back.*

(Crediful, n.d.).

## "PAY FOR DELETE" OFFER LETTER TEMPLATE

This is an agreement where you indicate you are willing to pay the amount owed in exchange for the missed payments or derogatory marks relating to the account to be removed from your credit report.

*[Original Creditor Name]*

*[Creditor Address]*

*[Creditor Phone Number]*

*[ACCOUNT NUMBER]*

*[Listed Amount Due]*

· · ·

DEAR [ORIGINAL CREDITOR *Name*]

REGARDING THE ABOVE-LISTED ACCOUNT, *it has been brought to my attention that you claim that I owe the listed amount shown above. While I accept no responsibility for ownership of this debt, I'm willing to compromise and offer a significant settlement amount in exchange for your agreement to the following:*

*Your agreement to the full and complete deletion of any past-due references pertaining to this account from all credit bureaus to which you report.*

*Your agreement that this payment constitutes a "paid in full" account, and not a "paid collection" or "settled account."*

*Your agreement that you will not attempt to sell or reassign the rights to this account to another third-party debt collection agency after payment has been received.*

*While I'm well aware that your purpose is to collect debts that you have obtained from original creditors, I am also aware that you are under no obligation to report any of these accounts to the credit bureaus.*

*That being said, your full cooperation in deleting this account in exchange for payment is appreciated.*

*When I receive signed documentation from your authorized representative on company letterhead stating that you agree* *to the terms above, I agree to pay $XXX.XX via certified funds – either cashier's check or money order. This payment will be sent to you via priority mail as soon as I receive the signed agreement.*

*Please be aware that this is not a renewed promise to pay. I do not claim responsibility for this debt, and I make no statement that I believe that this debt is valid or owed by me.*

*In the event that you do not agree with the resolution terms, I have offered above, I will move forward with my rights to request a full and complete verification and validation of this debt.*

*I LOOK FORWARD to a timely resolution of this matter.*

*REGARDS,*

*[Your Name]*

(Crediful, .n.d.).

GOODWILL LETTER TEMPLATE

Use the template below to appeal to your creditor for their understanding regarding late payments and ask them to consider either not reporting these to credit bureaus or removing them from your credit report.

· · ·

*[YOUR NAME]*

*[Your address]*

*[Your account number]*

*[Date]*

To Whom It May Concern:

Thank you for taking the time to read this letter. I'm writing because I noticed that my most recent credit report contains *[a late payment/payments]* reported on *[date/dates]* for my *[name of account]* account.

I want you to know that I understand my financial obligations, and if it weren't for *[circumstances that caused you to miss a payment]*, I'd have an excellent repayment record. I made a mistake in falling behind, but since then, *[description of how your circumstances have changed or how you've improved your money management]*. Since then, I've had a spotless record of on-time payments.

I'm planning to apply for *[a mortgage/auto loan/etc.]*, and it's come to my attention that the missed payment on my record could hurt my ability to qualify. I truly believe that it doesn't reflect my creditworthiness and commitment to repaying my debts. It would help me immensely if you could give me a second chance and make a goodwill adjustment to remove the late [payment/payments] on [date/dates].

THANK YOU FOR YOUR CONSIDERATION, and I hope you'll approve my request.

BEST,

[Your name]

(Nerd Wallet, 2021).

# AFTERWORD

Now that you are equipped with a multitude of tools and knowledge on how to repair your credit score, let's do a final recap of everything so that you can feel confident that you have what it takes to free yourself from debt.

At the outset, we established that insight into how the credit system works and how it affects your daily life is not common knowledge, but we use and need it so often that it even keeps a roof over our heads. The fear of the unknown soon became conquerable as we got to grips with that little number known as your credit score. This little number is not actually that little because we explored how you need a good credit score to get approved for life-changing financial moves like getting a mortgage, a student loan, or an auto loan.

We covered the five components that makeup how the FICO scoring system arrives at your credit score number, which are your payment history, balance owed, credit history length, credit mix, and amount of new credit. A good credit score ranges between 670 and 850. We then covered a few reasons why your credit score might currently be low. This may have been a sore point for you if a few of the bad credit habits we highlighted hit home for you, like not making your payments on time, using too much of your credit limit, or applying for too many types of new credit. Despite calling out your bad habits, we began to reveal the light at the end of the tunnel of debt by unpacking ways to repair your credit score and reduce your debt.

The first of these was to check your credit report from the three national credit bureaus, Experian, Equifax, and TransUnion. Checking your report takes you to the first and most successful solution, which is the 609 dispute letter. We ran through various other options, such as approaching a credit lawyer and the essential Simple Credit-Building Strategy. If anything, this strategy is what you need to take away from this book because implementing these good financial habits will change your life forever and lead you to financial freedom with a bit of patience. The strategy was fleshed out with simple tips you can try right away to increase your credit score, like disputing errors in your credit report; drawing up a monthly budget; keeping track of your debt-to-credit ratio; rate shopping for new credit; making use of automatic payments; managing different types of debt; removing hard inquiries from your credit report; avoiding late payments and charge-offs.

Almost every credit repair strategy we explored begins with thinking about how your financial actions can affect your credit score. The next steps usually involved checking your credit report for actual errors that you could successfully dispute, and every strategy ended with asking that you stick to trying to make your minimum monthly debt payments on time. Arming yourself with information to make the right decision about the credit you have, want to have, or want to get rid of is instrumental in ensuring the success of these strategies.

The goal of maintaining a healthy credit score is to manage your credit so that you are debt free and can make solid attempts at growing your income into investments and savings. Financial investments should not be considered a luxury reserved for a privileged few but should be a priority for your or your family's future because it's an investment in yourself.

There are many people who, just like you, felt that debt was just an inevitable fact of life and could never be overcome, but after what you've learned about how to repair your credit score, you know that debt can be conquered. You read a few success stories of people who thought they would never get their heads above water regarding their credit. They adopted strategies that suited them and were eventually able to invest in their future by buying homes or simply living debt-free. Breathing life back into your credit score and improving your financial status is completely possible if you select the best strategy for your individual situation based on what we've covered.

You've hopefully got a copy of your credit report in your hand as you read these closing words. If not, get online and grab a copy of it to review it for opportunities to get your credit score where you need it to be to be able to finance the life you've always dreamed of.

# REQUEST TO LEAVE REVIEW PAGE

# H elp Someone Else Breathe Easier Today!

YOU KNOW the weight of money troubles... and you've just learned a lot to help you breathe easier as you move forward. Now is your chance to help someone else do the same.

WITH JUST A FEW sentences on Amazon to let other readers know how this book has helped you, you can point new readers in the direction of the help they're looking for. You can be part of that weight being lifted for a complete stranger – and how good would that feel?!

**LEAVE A REVIEW!**

I can't thank you enough for your support. Together, we can help lift the weight of money troubles for thousands of people like you.

>>> Click here to leave your review on Amazon.

ALSO BY DIANA DONNELLY

Essential Advice for Buying Your First Home and Navigating
Through the Mortgage Loan Process

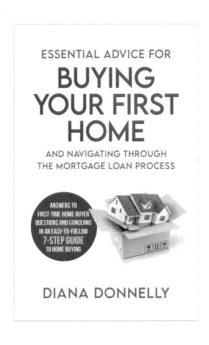

# GLOSSARY

**Account age**: An indication of how long your account has been open and the extent of your credit history. Creditors or lenders will assess the age of your credit accounts when reviewing credit applications or your creditworthiness.

**Adjustable rate**: When the interest rate of a loan can be changed or adjusted during the loan term.

**Annual percentage rate**: The yearly value of the loan or credit amount expressed as a percentage, including all fees and interest charged on the amount.

**Balance**: The latest update of the total amount that you still owe a creditor or bank from a loan.

**Bankruptcy**: A legal process where a debtor or borrower declares that they are unable to repay their debts, loans, or creditors.

**Charge-off**: The creditor has declared the account as a write-off or loss because of the debtor's continuous failure to pay off the debt. The account can be sold to a debt collector or debt buyer who will try to collect the outstanding balance from the debtor for their own profit.

**Collateral**: Made up of assets (movable or immovable) that the debtor declares that they are willing to give up to the creditor if the debtor fails to pay the debt. These assets are used to secure credit or a loan.

**Consumer dispute**: A consumer is entitled to approach a credit bureau to dispute any inaccuracies or assumed inaccuracies on their credit report. The company supplying the consumer's credit report must provide accurate, correct, and verified information.

**Credit bureau**: A credit reporting agency that creates reports from collecting credit information on people and companies. The Bureau then uses this information to generate a credit score. Equifax, Experian. and TransUnion are the three authorized credit bureaus operating within the USA.

**Credit card**: A card that works as an account providing revolving credit. The debtor, or borrower, uses the account to make purchases and repays the amount owed over an agreed upon time period. The creditor charges interest if the amount to be repaid is not paid on time.

**Credit history**: Data that summarizes your past and present credit commitments into a credit report. It includes your entire payment history, tax obligations, and any late payments.

**Credit inquiry**: Occurs when an authorized bank or other creditor reviews your credit report and credit history.

**Credit invisible**: A person with no credit history or data record with any of the three authorized credit bureaus.

**Credit limit**: The maximum amount of the creditor's money that the debtor is allowed to spend on each credit card or other revolving credit account that the debtor has. If the debtor spends more than the allowed credit limit, the creditor might suspend or cancel the account or charge fees beyond the repayment interest.

**Credit report**: Similar to your credit history, a credit report is an accurate and verified summary of your credit history that is prepared and issued by an authorized credit reporting entity. It includes every loan, credit card, mortgage, and any other credit facility you have used, repaid, or failed to repay.

**Credit score**: Your credit report is used to generate a score that ranges between 300 and 850 and indicates your creditworthiness, or how likely you are to pay back a loan. Your credit score is used by lenders to decide if they are willing to take the risk of allowing you to take a loan or credit with them.

**Debt-to-credit ratio**: Provides an indication of your financial stability and influences your credit score. It is calculated by dividing the total amount of your credit obligations by your available credit limit.

**Default**: A negative mark on your credit report that shows that you have failed to pay a debt.

**Delinquent**: The status of an account where the repayments have either been late or have not been paid at all. An account that is paid more than 30 days late is regarded as a delinquent account.

**Derogatory mark**: A negative mark on your credit report if you have continuously defaulted on payments or allowed your credit accounts to become delinquent accounts. This negatively affects your credit score and credit history.

**FICO score**: A category of credit score calculated by the Fair Isaac Corporation. The score is the most commonly used by creditors when assessing your creditworthiness and deciding if they are willing to take on the risk of lending you money.

**Fixed rate**: When the interest rate of a loan is set and cannot be changed or adjusted during the loan term.

**Good standing**: An account that the debtor has successfully repaid to the creditor within or before the allocated time period.

**Grace period**: A period during which the debtor can still make payments after their due date. This is a benefit provided by the creditor during which they will not charge late payment fees, create derogatory marks on your credit report, place you in default of your obligations, or cancel the loan.

**Hard inquiry**: Type of inquiry where a creditor asks a credit bureau for a copy of your credit report to assess your creditworthiness when you apply for credit. The creditor will have full sight of your financial history, and this type of inquiry can impact your credit score.

**Installment account**: A credit account or loan that must be repaid in regular installments. The creditor determines the repayment terms, and the debtor must make the installment payments on time to avoid being in default.

**Interest rate**: A percentage amount that the creditor charges the debtor to use the money borrowed.

**Late payment**: A payment made by the debtor after the payment due date. Continuous late payments on the same or on different loan repayments will become negative marks on your credit report and negatively impact your credit score.

**Line of credit**: This is similar to a credit limit, except that instead of being the maximum amount of money you can use on a credit card, it is the maximum amount of money you can borrow and use from a financial institution like a bank or investment house.

**Loan**: The simplest form of credit. It is money borrowed by a debtor from a creditor that is paid back with interest over a predetermined period of time.

**Net income**: Your monthly income after the government-required income taxes have been withdrawn from it.

**Net worth**: This represents your financial status and flexibility. It is calculated by subtracting your total liabilities from the total value of your assets.

**Principal amount**: The total amount of a loan, excluding interest.

**Public record data**: This data includes court judgments, legal disputes, and tax information that form part of the debtor's credit history. The data can impact the debtor's credit report.

**Revolving account**: A credit card is an example of this type of account. The maximum amount of credit the debtor has access to is set by the creditor. The outstanding balance owed by the debtor accumulates and rolls over each month. The debtor has to pay back a certain amount every month to avoid paying interest on the balance.

**Secured credit card**: The debtor secures the credit borrowed by paying a cash deposit for the entire or a portion of the credit limit. If the debtor misses any payments, they lose their cash deposit.

**Soft inquiry**: This type of inquiry does not impact your credit score and is usually used to make targeted marketing or promotional offers to you based on your financial habits. Potential creditors do not have sight of soft inquiries.

**Statute of limitations**: The time period within which a creditor can take legal action against you for not paying off your debt in time. For example, in certain states, a creditor must sue a defaulting debtor within four years (measured from when the loan agreement was signed) to avoid losing the principal debt amount.

**Trade line**: Trade lines in your credit report represent every account to give potential lenders a full picture of your financial status and habits. The companies, entities, and banks you took loans from, the dates these accounts were opened, the amount of credit you were provided, interest rates, your payment history, and any outstanding balances on those accounts will be contained in the trade line information for each credit account you have.

**Underwriting**: The task of creating appropriate loan or credit repayment terms that match the debtor's risk profile and financial habits. The loan's interest rate and its related fees will be determined during the underwriting process.

**Unsecured credit**: A loan that is granted based on the debtor's good standing and credit score, instead of being backed by collateral in the form of the debtor's assets.

# BIBLIOGRAPHY

*57 quotes about helping others.* (n.d.). Inspirational Words of Wisdom. https://www.wow4u.com/helping/

Bagtas, A. (2022, March 22). *What Is A 609 Letter And How Can It Help You? [In-Depth Guide].* Review 42. https://review42.com/resources/a-609-letter/

*Basic credit terms and definitions.* (n.d.). Protective. Retrieved September 18, 2022, from https://www.protective.com/learn/credit-glossary-terms-you-should-know

Black, M. (2021, December 22). *How to Remove Hard Inquiries from Credit Reports.* Nav.com. https://www.nav.com/blog/how-to-remove-hard-inquiries-from-credit-reports-526814/

Black, M. (2022, August 9). *609 Letter: The Free & Easy Credit Repair Tactic (Templates Included) - WealthFit.* Wealth Fit. https://wealthfit.com/articles/609-credit-repair/?itm_campaign_h=redirect&itm_medium_h=301&itm_source_h=%2Fmoney%2F609-credit-repair%2F#toc-609-credit-repair-sample

*Changes being made to Medical Debt Collections on Credit Reports.* (2022, April 27). American Financial Partners. https://financewithafp.com/blog/2022/04/27/changes-being-made-to-medical-debt-collections-on-credit-reports/

CBA Training Institute. (n.d.). *Glossary of Key Credit and Lending Terms.* CBA Training Institute. Retrieved September 19, 2022, from https://cbatraininginstitute.org/wp-content/uploads/2018/03/glossary_ofTerms.pdf

Consumer Financial Protection Bureau. (2020, September 1). *What are common credit report errors that I should look for on my credit report?* Consumer Financial Protection Bureau. https://www.consumerfinance.gov/ask-cfpb/what-are-common-credit-report-errors-that-i-should-look-for-on-my-credit-report-en-313/

Crouch, M. (2018, September 4). *13 Secrets Debt Collectors Won't Tell You.*

Reader's Digest. https://www.rd.com/list/13-things-a-debt-collector-wont-tell-you/

*Charge Off FAQs.* (n.d.-a). Equifax. Retrieved September 19, 2022, from https://www.equifax.com/personal/education/credit/report/charge-offs-faq/#:~:text=A%20charge%2Doff%20means%20a

*Credit Report Terminology.* (n.d.-b). Equifax. Retrieved September 18, 2022, from https://www.equifax.com/personal/education/credit/report/credit-report-terminology/

Dashiell, S., & Horner, M. (2022, August 30). *2022 Credit card debt and spending statistics in the US.* Finder. https://www.finder.com/credit-card-statistics#source

Dasko, M. (2022, July 25). *Get a Free Credit Report and Score (Honest).* Money under 30. https://www.moneyunder30.com/free-credit-report-score

DeNicola, L. (2021, May 5). *How Can I Remove Late Payments From My Credit Report?* Experian. https://www.experian.com/blogs/ask-experian/how-can-i-remove-late-payments-from-my-credit-report/

DeNicola, L. (2022, July 22). *How to remove late payments from your credit reports.* Credit Karma. https://www.creditkarma.com/advice/i/how-to-remove-late-payments

Dickler, J. (2020, February 25). *Here's how to improve your credit score right away.* CNBC. https://www.cnbc.com/2020/02/24/how-to-improve-your-credit-score-right-away.html

Dulcio, B. (2021, October 25). *How to Improve Your Credit Score: Tips & Tricks.* Debt.org. https://www.debt.org/credit/improving-your-score/

Egan, J. (2022, February 23). *The Main Types Of Debt And How To Handle Each.* Forbes. https://www.forbes.com/advisor/debt-relief/types-of-debt/

El Issa, E. (2021, June 16). *Should You Apply for Multiple Credit Cards at the Same Time?* Nerd Wallet. https://www.nerdwallet.com/article/credit-cards/apply-for-multiple-credit-cards-same-time

Frankel, M. (2019, October 12). *22% of Americans Don't Have a Credit Score -- Here's Why.* The Motley Fool. https://www.fool.com/the-ascent/credit-cards/articles/22-of-americans-dont-have-a-credit-score-heres-why/

Gill, L. L. (2021, June 10). *How to Fix Your Credit Score.* Consumer Reports. https://www.consumerreports.org/credit-scores-reports/how-to-fix-your-credit-score/

Gogol, F. (2022, August 30). *How to Remove Late Payments from a Credit Report.* Stilt. https://www.stilt.com/blog/2021/05/how-to-remove-late-payments-from-a-credit-report/

Green, T. (n.d.). *Top 6 Hacks on How To Build Credit Fast.* Life Hack. Retrieved September 18, 2022, from https://www.lifehack-.org/448813/the-best-ways-to-build-credit-fast#top-6-hacks-on-how-to-build-credit-fast

*Household Debt and Credit Report - Federal Reserve Bank of New York.* (2022). Federal Reserve Bank of New York. https://www.newyork-fed.org/microeconomics/hhdc

*How Many Credit Inquiries Is Too Many?* (2021, June 24). Capital One. https://www.capitalone.com/learn-grow/money-manage-ment/how-many-credit-inquiries-is-too-many/

*How are FICO Scores Different than Credit Scores?* (n.d.). My FICO. Retrieved September 19, 2022, from https://www.myfico.-com/credit-education/fico-scores-vs-credit-scores

Holmes, T. E. (2021, July 8). *Credit card race, age, gender statistics.* Credit-Cards. https://www.creditcards.com/statistics/race-age-gender-statistics/

Horymski, C. (2022, February 22). *What Is the Average Credit Score in the U.S.?* Experian. https://www.experian.com/blogs/ask-exper-ian/what-is-the-average-credit-score-in-the-u-s/

*How to build and maintain a solid credit history and score.* (2020, March 3). US Bank. https://www.usbank.com/financialiq/manage-your-household/establish-credit/how-to-build-and-maintain-a-solid-credit-history-and-score.html

*Investment Disclaimers – The Best Free Disclaimer Template!* (n.d.). Disclaimer Template. Retrieved September 19, 2022, from https://www.disclaimertemplate.net/investment-disclaimers/

Irby, L. (2021, October 31). *Reasons You Should Not Close A Credit Card.*

The Balance. https://www.thebalancemoney.com/credit-cards-you-should-never-close-960970

Irby, L. (2022, May 18). *How to Remove Negative Credit Report Entries Yourself.* The Balance. https://www.thebalancemoney.com/remove-negative-credit-report-960734

J.D, N. W. (2021, December 17). *609 Letter: What It Is & How It Works.* Upsolve. https://upsolve.org/learn/609-letter/

JP Morgan Chase & Co. (n.d.). *How automatic payments can help your credit score | Chase.* Chase. Retrieved September 18, 2022, from https://www.chase.com/personal/credit-cards/education/credit-score/how-automatic-payments-help-credit-score

Kagan, J. (2020, August 11). *Introduction to Re-Aging Debt.* Investopedia. https://www.investopedia.com/terms/r/reaging-debt.asp#:~:text=There%20is%20one%20good%20type

Kiyosaki, R. (2020, January 13). *10 Steps To Improve Your Credit Score.* Paradigm Press, LLC. https://paradigm.press/2020/01/13/10-steps-to-improve-your-credit-score/

Lake, R. (2021, June 3). *Can You Get Charge-Offs Erased From Your Credit Reports?* Investopedia. https://www.investopedia.com/how-do-i-remove-charge-offs-from-my-credit-5075534

Legal, P. (2022, April 12). *Should I Hire A Credit Lawyer?* Pride Legal. https://pridelegal.com/hire-credit-lawyer/

Leonhardt, M. (2020, December 17). *A poor credit score affects more than just getting a loan or credit card.* CNBC. https://www.cnbc.com/2020/12/17/poor-credit-scores-affect-more-than-just-getting-a-loan-or-credit-card.html

Luthi, B. (2021, January 12). *Credit Repair: How to "Fix" Your Credit Yourself - Experian.* Experian. https://www.experian.com/blogs/ask-experian/credit-education/improving-credit/credit-repair/

Luthi, B., & Jayakumar, A. (2019, October 31). *Lenders Look at More Than Just Your Credit Score.* Nerd Wallet. https://www.nerdwallet.com/article/finance/mortgage-lenders-credit-score-interest-rate

Martucci, B. (2021, September 14). *What Hurts and Affects Your Credit Score? - 9 Factors & Errors to Fix.* Money Crashers. https://www.moneycrashers.com/what-hurts-affects-your-credit-score-factors/

Masters Credit Consultants. (n.d.). *10 Most Common Negative Items On*

*Your Credit Report.* Masters Credit Consultants. Retrieved September 18, 2022, from https://www.masterscredit.-com/2020/12/21/10-most-common-negative-items-on-your-credit-report/

Millstein, S. (2021, December 1). *FCRA Section 609 Credit Repair Method [Sample "609 Letters"].* Credit Repair Expert. https://www.creditre-pairexpert.org/609-letter/

Muller, C. (2022, June 17). *14 Helpful Tips for Maintaining a Good Credit Score.* Money under 30. https://www.moneyunder30.com/tips-for-maintaining-a-good-credit-score

Nerd Wallet. (2021, February 10). *How to Write a Goodwill Letter to Remove a Late Payment.* Nerd Wallet. https://www.nerdwallet.-com/article/finance/goodwill-letter

O'Shea, B. (2021, October 19). *Why Is My Credit Score Low, Even Though I Pay My Bills on Time?* Nerd Wallet. https://www.nerdwallet.-com/article/finance/why-credit-score-is-low

O'Shea, B. (2022a, March 2). *7 Ways to Build Credit Fast.* Nerd Wallet. https://www.nerdwallet.com/article/finance/raise-credit-score-fast

O'Shea, B. (2022b, March 16). *How Does a Late Payment Affect Your Credit?* Nerd Wallet. https://www.nerdwallet.com/article/finance/late-bill-payment-reported

O'Shea, B., & Barroso, A. (2022, July 26). *How to Report Your Rent to Credit Bureaus.* Nerd Wallet. https://www.nerdwallet.com/arti-cle/finance/rent-reporting-services

Okerlund, A. (2021, May 7). *3 Credit Repair Success Stories and Tips That Will Inspire You.* Best Company. https://bestcompany.com/credit-repair/blog/3-credit-repair-success-stories-and-tips-that-will-inspire-you

Orem, T. (2022, January 18). *How to Claim a Tax Deduction for Medical Expenses in 2022.* Nerd Wallet. https://www.nerdwallet.com/arti-cle/taxes/medical-expense-tax-deduction

Porter, K. (2022, June 8). *What is a derogatory mark on your credit reports?* Credit Karma. https://www.creditkarma.com/advice/i/what-does-derogatory-mean

Rosenberg, E. (2021, October 13). *FCRA: Fair Credit Reporting Act.* Credit Karma. https://www.creditkarma.com/advice/i/fcra

Sandberg, E. (2022, February 22). *609 Letter Template & How to File a Credit Dispute.* Bad Credit. https://www.badcredit.org/how-to/609-letter/

Seemann, K. (2022, June 17). *7 Tips To Increase Your Chase Credit Limit (With Tips for Denial).* Upgraded Points. https://www. upgradedpoints.com/credit-cards/increase-chase-credit-limit/

Serio, A. (2022, January 18). *Personal Loans: Compare Trusted Online Lenders in 2022 | Finder.* Finder. https://www.finder.com/personal-loans

Take Charge America Team. (n.d.). *Free Resources to Help Improve Your Credit.* Take Charge America. Retrieved September 18, 2022, from https://www.takechargeamerica.org/free-resources-to-help-improve-your-credit/

Terrell, S. (2021, March 12). *14 negative items that can affect your credit report defined.* Finder.. https://www.finder.com/negative-items-on-credit-report

Timestaff. (2014, May 26). *What Is My Credit Score, and How Is It Calculated?* Money. https://money.com/collection-post/what-is-my-credit-score/

Tretina, K. (2019, June 27). *What Is Piggybacking Credit?* Experian. https://www.experian.com/blogs/ask-experian/what-is-piggy-backing-credit/

VanSomeren, L. (2021, May 18). *How To Fix Your Credit In 7 Easy Steps.* Forbes. https://www.forbes.com/advisor/credit-score/how-to-fix-your-credit/

Yera, A., Rodríguez, N., & Agostini, A. (2022, July 7). *How to Remove Negative Items From Your Credit Report.* Money. https://money.com/get-items-removed-from-credit-report/

*What are the Different Types of Consumer Debt?* (n.d.-d). Equifax. Retrieved September 19, 2022, from https://www.equifax.com/personal/education/debt-management/types-of-consumer-debts/

*What is A Credit Score?* (n.d.-c). Equifax. Retrieved September 19, 2022, from https://www.equifax.com/personal/education/credit/score/what-is-a-credit-score/

*What Are Inquiries On Your Credit Report?* (n.d.). Experian. Retrieved September 19, 2022, from https://www.experian.com/blogs/askexperian/credit-education/report-basics/hard-vs-soft-inquiries-on-your-credit-report/

*Sample Debt Validation Letter.* (n.d.-a). Crediful. Retrieved September 19, 2022, from https://www.crediful.com/debt-validation-letter/

*Sample "Pay for Delete" Letters.* (n.d.-b). Crediful. Retrieved September 19, 2022, from https://www.crediful.com/pay-for-delete-letter/

## IMAGE REFERENCES

Barbhuiya, T. (2021a). *Man hand open an empty wallet with copy space* [Image]. Unsplash. https://unsplash.com/photos/3aGZ7a97qwA

Barbhuiya, T. (2021b). *Photo by Towfiqu Barbhuiya on Unsplash* [Image]. Unsplash. https://unsplash.com/photos/0ITvgXAU5Oo

Braňo. (2021). *3D visualization* [Image]. Unsplash. https://unsplash.com/photos/heYdDdq0cbE

Bughdaryan, S. (2021). *Brown wooden chess piece on brown book* [Image]. Unsplash. https://unsplash.com/photos/e11Oa3kvx4c

Chuangchoem, A. (2017). *Black analog alarm clock at 7:01* [Image]. Pexels. https://www.pexels.com/photo/black-analog-alarm-clock-at-7-01-359989/

Clker-Free-Vector-Images. (n.d.). *Circle shape quadrants sectors* [Image]. Pixabay. Retrieved September 19, 2022, from https://pixabay.com/vectors/circle-shape-quadrants-sectors-25937/

Grabowska, K. (2020a). *Hourglass near heap of American dollars* [Image]. Pexels. https://www.pexels.com/photo/hourglass-near-heap-of-american-dollars-4386235/

Grabowska, K. (2020b). *Crop anonymous woman working with documents sitting at table with computer* [Image]. Pexels. https://www.pexels.com/photo/crop-anonymous-woman-working-with-documents-sitting-at-table-with-computer-4491456/

Graham, S. (2015). *Sign here* [Image]. Unsplash. https://unsplash.com/photos/OQMZwNd3ThU

Henwood, L. (2015). *Person stepping on blue stairs* [Image]. Unsplash. https://unsplash.com/photos/7_kRuX1hSXM

Kusuma, A. (2021). *Success hitting target aim goal achievement concept background - three darts in bull's eye close up. red three darts arrows in the target center business goal concept* [Image]. Unsplash. https://unsplash.com/photos/RjqCk9MqhNg

Lusina, A. (2020). *Person choosing document in folder* [Image]. Pexels. https://www.pexels.com/photo/person-choosing-document-in-folder-4792285/

Micheile dot com. (2020). *Green plant in clear glass cup* [Image]. Unsplash. https://unsplash.com/photos/SoT4-mZhyhE

Otto, N. (2018). *Close-up photography of magnifying glass* [Image]. Pexels. https://www.pexels.com/photo/close-up-photography-of-magnifying-glass-906055/

Our Life in Pixels. (2020). *Building a Jenga tower* [Image]. Unsplash. https://unsplash.com/photos/Ys78stblUyY

Pasqual, A. (2017). *Until debt tear us apart* [Image]. Unsplash. https://unsplash.com/photos/Olki5QpHxts

Piacquadio, A. (2020). *Young troubled woman using laptop at home* [Image]. Pexels. https://www.pexels.com/photo/young-troubled-woman-using-laptop-at-home-3755755/

Pixabay. (2017). *Blue Mastercard on denim pocket* [Image]. Pexels. https://www.pexels.com/photo/blue-master-card-on-denim-pocket-164571/

Regularguy.eth. (2021). *Photo by Regularguy.eth on Unsplash* [Image]. Unsplash. https://unsplash.com/photos/K_3UV1ZFcJ0

Sneddon, R. (2020). *Jigsaw* [Image]. Unsplash. https://unsplash.com/photos/sWlDOWk0Jp8

Made in United States
Troutdale, OR
12/07/2023

15454059R00106